# DISASTER 1906
## THE SAN FRANCISCO EARTHQUAKE AND FIRE

At 5:12 A.M. on the morning of April 18, 1906, San Francisco rested in tranquility, awaiting the coming of another usual bustling day. Two minutes later the city was the scene of carnage, streets uptorn, houses crumpled, water mains burst, gas and electricity cut off. An earthquake, striking in two giant tremors, had begun what was to become an epic of destruction. But it was only a foretaste of things to come. When the quake had had its turn, fire took over. Interweaving the many threads of the disaster, this book recreates the hour-by-hour suspense of three days that saw a city laid to waste, a half-billion dollars of property destroyed, and a quarter of a million people made homeless. But it tells, too, of the courage of those people, of the aid rushed from all corners of the nation and the globe, and of the amazing process of rebuilding that began even as the ashes were still smoldering. From those ashes rose a new San Francisco, and from the terror of earthquake and fire emerged an inspiring example of the indomitable spirit of man.

# DISASTER 1906

*The San Francisco Earthquake and Fire*

*by*

**Edward F. Dolan, Jr.**

ILLUSTRATED WITH MAPS AND
PHOTOGRAPHS

*Julian Messner*    *New York*

The author wishes to acknowledge permission to quote passages from the following books:

*The Earth Shook, The Sky Burned* by William Knox Bronson. Copyright © 1959 by William Knox Bronson. Reprinted by permission of Doubleday & Company, Inc., New York

*The Great Earthquake and Fire: San Francisco, 1906* by John Castillo Kennedy. Copyright © 1963 by John Castillo Kennedy. Reprinted by permission of William Morrow and Company, New York

*Bonanza Inn* by Oscar Lewis and Carroll D. Hall. Copyright © 1939 by Alfred A. Knopf, Inc. Reprinted by permission of Alfred A. Knopf, Inc., New York

*Photographs Courtesy The Society of California Pioneers*

Printed in the United States of America

Library of Congress Catalog Card No. 67-21621

# CONTENTS

*This book is for Irene Rollins*

# DISASTER 1906

## THE SAN FRANCISCO EARTHQUAKE
## AND FIRE

# Chapter One

## WEDNESDAY, APRIL 18, 1906

5:12 A.M.

A MOMENT OF QUIET lay over the city—a moment of quiet between the boisterous night and the busy day. Most of San Francisco's 450,000 people were asleep. Those who had gone to the theater or the opera last evening and then dined and danced the rest of the night away were just now in bed and beginning to doze. Just settling down, too, were those who had squandered the dark hours in the saloons along the Barbary Coast or the gambling parlors of Chinatown. Thousands more, all the laborers and clerks and merchants and housewives and children who were the backbone of this young city by the Pacific, were burrowing a little deeper into their pillows for a last few minutes before rising to the new day.

Here and there, a few people were already up. Wisps of smoke were spiraling from chimneys everywhere. Familiar cooking odors were in the air—the aromas of coffee heating and bacon frying. Over to the east, beyond the Ferry Building at the foot of Market Street, the sky was blue-pink with the dawn. On Market Street itself, which fell wide and spear straight through the heart of the city, a policeman walked, slowly, tiredly. He was thinking that he would soon be done with his night's patrol and that, after

*11*

he had slept a time, he would work in his garden. All the street lights had been switched off four minutes ago. The temperature was just under fifty degrees.

5:12:05 A.M.

Three miles from where the policeman walked—beyond the hills that loomed above Market to the north and then curved round to cross it at Twin Peaks far to the southwest —a quiet ocean breeze was coming through the Golden Gate and thinning the low fog that had spread itself over the Bay at midnight. Near the crest of Telegraph Hill, an Italian housewife stood at her kitchen window and watched the base of Alcatraz Island emerge from the dissolving mist halfway to the Gate. She felt a little thrust of pride for her home, which occupied the top floor of a three-story wooden apartment building. It was not the finest place in the world, she knew, but perched here above the northeast corner of the peninsula where the city had been built, it took a backseat to no other so far as the view was concerned. With just a turn of her head, she could follow the Bay along San Francisco's northern shore to that point where its gray-green waters fanned out north and south— north to sweep past faraway hills and towns, south to drop past the eastern face of the city with its Ferry Building and endless wharves. Out of the corner of her eye, she could see the start of those wharves. Thrusting straight out from the land, they looked like the rungs of a ladder that some giant had flung down flat and then left behind.

She sighed, pulled her woolen robe tighter about her, and walked through to her parlor where the view from her front window, though different, was just as magnificent.

Here, she looked down on the very core of San Francisco.

The Ferry Building was on her left now. Market started its southwesterly run through the city from there, and she followed it for two blocks to the produce district where her husband was already at work this day; the district sprawled north of Market along Davis and Front Streets, and its brick buildings were piled high with meats and vegetables and fruits awaiting deliveries to shops all over town. It was surrounded, she saw, by an area of wholesale stores and offices that merged with several blocks of retail stores on its west side. They, in turn, ran into the city's financial district on Montgomery Street. Back to Market her eyes went, moving on until she came to a series of fine buildings—the elegant Palace Hotel at New Montgomery; the eighteen-story *Call* Building and its squat neighbor, the *Examiner* Building, at Third Street; and the great Emporium department store between Fifth and Sixth. Clustered about them by the dozen were others, all the offices, stores, restaurants and theaters of the downtown district.

Spread out on their far side were the frame houses, apartments, hotels and boardinghouses of the shabby area which all San Franciscans called "South of the Slot." The nickname was an old one, given because the area lay south of the shallow trench that had housed the cable for the old Market Street cable cars. She was glad that she did not live there; its people were even poorer than her own neighbors. She thought it an unhealthy place. Its buildings were all pressed too close together, and too much of it was built on fill earth that had been dumped over mosquito-filled marshland.

Her gaze returned to Market and then went just north of it. There, in the far distance, she could make out the

CENTRAL·
SAN FRANCISCO:

MAJOR STREETS,
BUILDINGS, AREAS

A. TELEGRAPH HILL
B. RUSSIAN HILL
C. NOB HILL
D. CHINATOWN
E. PRODUCE, RETAIL AREAS
F. 'SOUTH OF SLOT' AREA

1. FERRY BUILDING
2. HALL OF JUSTICE
3. PORTSMOUTH SQUARE
4. UNION SQUARE
5. ST. FRANCIS HOTEL
6. CITY HALL
7. POST OFFICE
8. MINT
9. THE EMPORIUM
10. CALL BUILDING
11. PALACE HOTEL

road beginnings of Van Ness Avenue. It stretched north
east intervening hills all the way from Market to the Bay,
dividing the central section of the city from the mixture of
middle-class and wealthy neighborhoods that stretched

westward over and between hills and past sprawling Golden Gate Park to the Pacific beaches. About two blocks to the housewife's side of Van Ness, the City Hall dome thrust itself against the dawn sky. Closer to her was Nob Hill, its crown emblazoned with some of the mightiest homes in California; built into its southern foot were Union Square and the St. Francis Hotel. Closer still, set against the eastern slopes of the hill, were the narrow streets of Chinatown with the brick towers of Old St. Mary's Church looming above them. North of Nob Hill, and almost directly west of her own Telegraph Hill, was Russian Hill with its middle-class homes and tidily maintained yards.

The housewife lingered over the panorama for another moment before returning to her kitchen. Back at her sink, she decided to let the children stay in bed a little longer than usual this morning. They had been awake most of the night, crowding about this very window to stare, wide-eyed, down at the fire that had roared through the California Cannery Company warehouse in the North Beach area. She could see the warehouse now, a blackened shell. To her eye, it was the only ugly thing in view as a new and sunny spring day broke over this city that was as hilly as her native Rome.

5:12:15 A.M.

Enrico Caruso lay asleep in one of the most expensive suites at the Palace Hotel. He slept contentedly, for he had just lived through one of his finest moments as a singer. Last night, with a touring company from New York's Metropolitan Opera, he had sung the role of Don José in

Bizet's *Carmen*. He had been the hit of the evening, taking one curtain call after another from three thousand cheering San Franciscans and granting a series of dressing room interviews to local reporters before going on to a supper party at Zinkind's Restaurant. He was to sing again at the San Francisco Opera House before returning to New York.

In an apartment near Van Ness Avenue, a twenty-four-year-old actor named John Barrymore lay half asleep on a living room divan. The apartment belonged to a young man whom he had met at a party close on midnight after watching Caruso's performance. The young man had remarked that he owned a collection of Chinese porcelain and, finding Barrymore interested, had invited him home to see several vases that had arrived just that day from Shanghai. Since the hour was late, Barrymore accepted an invitation to "camp" there the rest of the night, thus saving himself the trouble of trying to hail a cab back to his own rooms at the St. Francis Hotel.

The actor shifted restlessly because he knew that he must be up and away early. He was sailing at noon today for Australia, where he was to open in a play, and he had some last-minute packing to do.

Near the financial district, Fire Chief Dennis Sullivan lay in exhausted sleep in his apartment on the third floor of the Bush Street firehouse. He had returned just an hour or so ago from the fire at the California Cannery Company warehouse. The blaze had destroyed the block-long warehouse, but because there was little or no wind, it had not spread to other buildings in the crowded North Beach area where many of San Francisco's Italian people lived. Outside and one story up from the Sullivan apartment, a cluster of chimneys atop the California Theater and Hotel next door loomed gray-black in the dawn.

5:12:20 A.M.

A newspaper editor named Barrett stood with three fellow
workers outside the *Examiner* Building at Third and
Market. They had just finished putting today's edition of
their paper to press, and now they were waiting for the
streetcars that would soon come trundling up Market
Street to take them home.

Barrett ran his mind back over the night's work. He
nodded with satisfaction. The *Examiner* would carry its
fair share of good stories when it arrived on doorsteps and
at newsstands. There was the latest report on that mine
disaster that had claimed one hundred lives at Calais,
France. There was an item that said Los Angeles had collected $10,000 for the victims of last week's earthquake in
Formosa. And there was an on-the-spot report of yesterday's meeting in Judge W. W. Morrow's chambers to form
committees to take care of any similar emergencies that
might occur here in San Francisco, historically a favorite
target for earthquakes and fires.

Barrett yawned and looked toward the Ferry Building
spire, with the dawn now strong all about it. Behind the
building, he knew, the ferryboats were being fired for the
first of their daily runs across the Bay to Oakland, Berkeley, Alameda and Richmond. He heard one of his friends
start to tell a joke.

He turned to listen.

It struck.

First, there was the rumble, faraway and indefinite for a
split second, a massive train rushing toward an unknown
somewhere in the great distance. But, in the next split
second, it had direction to it. It was thundering in across

the Bay from the north, closing in all around, blotting
out every other sound of the dawn. Then it slammed into
the city, rolled through its hills, and came up under its
flatlands and marshes, and the movement was there with it,
snapping the earth back and forth.

That first movement was horizontal, as if a monster ter-
rier, as one man later wrote, had suddenly caught San
Francisco in its jaws and was "shaking it like a rat." But
it was quickly joined by a vertical movement, one that
turned the ground into a rolling sea. Barrett staggered into
the street. He glimpsed his friends reeling drunkenly, one
grabbing at a lamppost. Overhead, the buildings were
doing a sort of crazy dance against the sky.

There was a crash nearby as a display window fell away
from a store. Barrett was now turned toward the Ferry
Building. He saw a man running along the sidewalk about
a block away. A cornice of a building broke away, shot
downward and smashed through the sidewalk, crushing the
small figure. Clouds of dust boiled up two stories. Chunks
of concrete flew in all directions, as if they were grapeshot
fired from a cannon.

What Barrett was seeing was only a fraction of the havoc
beginning to grip central San Francisco. All along Market
Street and wherever else there were streetcar tracks, the
electric lines above them sagged, some parting in showers
of blue-green sparks. The tracks themselves were twisted to
one side or the other; some snapped apart and curled upward into ten-foot-high arcs. Underground water pipes
were crushed or sheared off by the moving earth, and
water bubbled to the surface and ran along the gutters.
Every electric light in the city went dead. Down at the
harbor, the Long Wharf caved in, dumping into the Bay
thousands of tons of coal belonging to the Southern Pacific

Railroad. Far to the south, two ships at the Hunter's Point drydock fell away from their scaffolding.

In his fifth-floor suite at the Palace Hotel, Enrico Caruso sat bolt upright in bed, awakened by a rain of falling plaster and the thunder of the earthquake. His bed staggered toward the center of the room. A table lamp crashed to the floor. A painting rattled against the wall opposite him, tilted itself and then fell, its glass face shattering.

Elsewhere in the hotel, another guest came awake as he was thrown to the floor. Blindly, he clawed at the bed. All he could think of was the six hundred dollars' worth of gold in a pouch beneath the pillows. He found the pouch, struggled to his feet and began to search frenziedly for his clothes.

On Telegraph Hill, the Italian housewife stumbled against her sink. She saw a chunk of red flash past her window. A breath later, the upper four feet of her chimney buried itself intact in the narrow backyard below. Everywhere, the same scene repeated itself countless times as chimneys snapped away at their bases and hurled themselves clear of houses or crashed down through rooftops. Many, however, with their bricks mortared with the sandy loam from San Francisco's beaches, simply disintegrated, and their bricks dropped in a thundering rain; some clattered down sloping roofs, others flew through windows, and still others dropped in heaps in streets and backyards. Later estimates held that ninety-five out of every one hundred chimneys in the city were damaged in the quake.

Down with the chimneys came the fronts of apartments, boardinghouses, stores and hotels throughout the downtown district. Revealed were terrified people thrust upright in bed or transfixed in the act of washing or eating. But they were the lucky ones, those people who lost just

the fronts of their homes, far luckier than those trapped
when entire buildings collapsed. Hardest hit was the vast
South of the Slot area, with its hundreds of flimsily built
structures. On lower Third Street, the outer walls of the
Denver House Hotel caved in and the roof subsided
through two floors to the ground, killing two sleepers and
injuring eighteen others. Over on Fourth Street, the Royal
Hotel fell apart. Three boardinghouses came down in two
separate blocks on Fifth Street, followed by the Porter
House on Sixth. A short distance down Sixth, the five-story
Brunswick Hotel collapsed in on its three hundred rooms.

Next hardest hit was the produce district, its one- and
two-story brick buildings instantly coming apart. Truck
horses reared back in a frenzy as drivers tried to whip them
away from collapsing walls. By the ton, bricks crashed
down on the wagons laden for market, crushing them,
their drivers and their teams. Two drivers sprinted away
from a tottering wall. They turned back to save a horse
and wagon left behind. They died with the animal under
the rubble of the wall.

In the surrounding wholesale district and the retail area
next door, the destruction was just as complete. The fronts
fell away from one store and office after another, and the
roofs came down behind them. Only the fact that the hour
was too early for business kept the death toll here to almost
nothing, while people died by the dozen in the produce
and the South of the Slot areas. At the harbor, a steel
girder broke away from a pier shed and smashed down
across the bows of the steamer *San Pablo*. The steamer
settled in the mud. Brown water crashed into her main
deck salons.

On the third floor of the Bush Street firehouse, Chief

Dennis Sullivan threw back his blankets and jumped to his feet. His wife's bedroom was down the hall from his, and his first thought was to reach her. Outside, the chimneys on the roof of the California Theater and Hotel broke away from their base. They crashed down through the station and turned the hall into a gaping hole. Sullivan threw open his bedroom door and plunged two stories to the rubble below. Critically injured about the chest and head, he was to die five days later. Miraculously, his wife escaped unharmed in the tragedy.

The quake was now thirty seconds old. Suddenly—with even less warning than it had given at its start—it quieted itself. The ground was strangely still again. A heavy silence gripped the city, so heavy that one survivor later wrote, "you could almost feel it." The silence and the stillness held for ten seconds.

While those seconds slipped away, San Franciscans everywhere drew in a great trembling breath and then let it go on a sigh of relief. In the downtown area and all through the South of the Slot blocks, people were so stunned and terrified that they could not comprehend what had happened. They could only think that they were still alive. Reactions were more varied in the western neighborhoods out beyond Van Ness. Here, the quake had not been so severe, and in several places it had failed to rouse some heavy sleepers. Too, sturdy construction out here had protected the people. Granted, many chimneys were down and crockery was smashed, but the homes were still intact and most people were able to grin and say that their city had lived through just one more trembler. Quakes had been coming along regularly for years now; a couple of them had been dandies, but most had been light,

and some had hardly been felt at all. This one, they
agreed, had probably lasted a little longer than last December's shake. . . .

A fresh convulsion, far worse than the one of a breath
ago, gripped the city. All the twisting movement and the
jarring sound were back again. East Street (now called the
Embarcadero), which ran down the length of the harbor,
became a cobblestone sea, rising and falling in a series of
three-foot-high waves. Newspaperman Barrett and his
friends were thrown flat on Market while the *Examiner*
Building tottered above them. Barrett later wrote that the
cobblestones in the street seemed to be popping up from
their foundations. Blocks north of Barrett, the dome of the
Hall of Justice at Portsmouth Square sagged. The front
wall of the brick jail on nearby Broadway fell into the
street.

Far west, near Van Ness, on Larkin Street, a man was
trying to pull himself up from his hands and knees. He
stared in horror at the City Hall, which was built in a
triangle formed by Market, Larkin and McAllister Streets.
The disintegration of its six-million-dollar bulk had begun
with the first shock, and now the process was completing
itself. He saw the great pillars along the border of its circu-
lar front porch topple in a swirling cloud of mortar dust,
burying the tramps who slept huddled there each night.
Behind them, looking like a nightmare waterfall, came sections of the upper story walls, leaving behind naked
girders exposed right to the dome.

The man was up and running. The noise of the building coming apart was deafening. Behind him, a great col-
umn fell across Larkin and crashed into an apartment
house. The man stopped dead in his tracks at Market and

Larkin. He watched the dome of the Majestic Theater just along Market cave in on itself.

The city's detention hospital was located in the basement of City Hall. When the building above came down, the walls and ceilings of the hospital collapsed about Mrs. Kane, who was the matron there. With her starched bonnet askew and her face caked with dust, she scrambled through the rubble, bumped against a tilted door frame and ran out into the morning air. Behind her came John McLean, the policeman on duty in the wing. They dashed clear of the mortar and plaster raining down from the City Hall dome. Then, panting, they stopped to stare at each other, a horrible realization showing in their faces. They had left six insane patients behind, each locked in a padded cell.

Nearby, City Emergency Hospital caved in, burying doctors, nurses and patients in a mass of broken doorways, ceiling plaster and snapped roof beams.

For many, the ground itself now seemed to be coming apart. Much of San Francisco, particularly the South of the Slot district, was built on fill earth. In fact, at one time, the Bay had come up on both sides of Market for more than a quarter of a mile beyond where the harbor now lay. Through the years, for the purposes of housing construction, the marshes and shallows here had been covered over with sand and debris and earth, sometimes without bothering to haul away the remains of ships that had first come to San Francisco back in the Gold Rush days of 1849. The quake was too much for this weak foundation. It trembled like so much jelly and then, in one spot after another, gave way. In South of the Slot, it joined with the flimsy construction to make the devastation monstrous. At points along Mission Street, which runs parallel to Market one block south, the ground sank to a depth of five feet. Next to the Post Office, at Seventh Street and Mission, it dropped six feet.

A fleeing guest ran across the lobby of the Palace Hotel to the main entrance, his nightshirt tucked into a pair of trousers. He stared out onto Market Street and screamed, for he was certain that he saw the cobbled roadway split open along its middle and swallow up hundreds of plunging cattle. Later, he refused to change his mind about what he had "seen," not even when searchers could find no evidence of major seam marks in the street, and not even when they told him that no cattle had come charging through the heart of the city in the first place.

But elsewhere, there was nothing imaginary about the collapsing ground. It gave way beneath a new apartment building that had been placed on fill across an empty stream bed at Valencia and Nineteenth Avenues, about a mile west of the downtown district. The building sank until its second story was level with the street. Nearby, where old Willow Creek had been filled in for housing, the four-story Valencia Hotel slid forward into the street, its roof dropping and carrying its upper walls inward so that it compressed itself into a one-story building. Later reports held that between twenty and eighty people died in the wreckage. Next door, a two-story boardinghouse was left tilted at a twenty-degree angle.

Just as dangerous as the fill earth were the slopes north of Market Street. In several places, the earth split and then fell away from beneath hillside homes, and they went sliding down through their rear fences and into the backyards below. High up on Union Street, a streetcar track twisted itself six feet to one side, and the bank beneath it subsided and flowed down and away, leaving the track suspended in the air.

By now, people everywhere were beginning to dash into the streets. Most were in nightdress and barefoot. They ran blindly into the swirling mortar dust and the continuing rain of falling bricks, stones and plaster. They bumped into each other, often knocking one another down, sometimes stopping dazedly to help each other up. They cut their feet on shattered glass; they fainted; and some fell to their knees in weeping prayer.

But most San Franciscans were still inside their homes, so shocked that they could not move. Others could not pull open doors that had been jammed when their homes were knocked out of kilter. Still others were lurching from room to room to collect the members of their families. One man later wrote that he thought only of gathering his wife and children about him "so that when the house went down we should all go together." And everywhere in the areas hardest hit, there were those who could not escape because they were pinned beneath collapsed walls and ceilings.

But there was not fear or panic or tragedy everywhere. This second shock had been just as kind to some of the city's western neighborhoods as had been the first one. And so some people still slept on. Others, coming awake, dismissed the whole thing as "just another shake" and went back to sleep. Some made their way through dancing chairs and tables and fallen wardrobe cabinets to stand in doorways, which, they knew, would protect them from falling debris and dropping ceilings. Others crawled beneath their beds. One husband later recalled that he jumped up to stand with his back pressed against a wardrobe cabinet so that it would not fall across his wife in bed.

Even where the quake was hitting hardest, there was not

always panic. A science teacher at breakfast calmly watched the swinging chandelier above his dining room table, trying to judge the growing intensity of the quake by noting the increasing arc described by the chandelier. John Barrymore sat up on the divan in his friend's living room and watched the Chinese porcelain from Shanghai crash all about him.

Throughout the city, the quake worked its way to its end. Far west of the downtown district, roadways split open in Golden Gate Park and trees jumped and twisted at wild angles. Some tore their roots from the sandy soil and toppled over on their sides. Wooden houses along a stretch of Dore Street south of Market were jarred into a series of insane angles; some were left leaning to one side or the other; some were shoved backward, some forward; the stairways leading up from the sidewalk broke away from their front porches. Fire hydrants snapped their bolts in several neighborhoods and shot water forty feet into the air. Huge headstones fell over in every one of the city's cemeteries. A side wall peeled away from the second story of the Mission Street police station, and the dome above crashed down after it. A few blocks away, at Third and Mission, a fireman put his head out a window at his station; he was killed by a piece of falling cornice. Close by, the wall fronting a line of tenements buckled inward, giving the building the look of a great brown dog gone back on its haunches.

Then, as if the ground were suddenly tired of all the fury in it, the frenzied movement began to subside and the deafening roar to fade, until, for a final second or so, there were a few last spasmodic twists, as though a giant chest was trying to catch its breath. Finally, the spring morning was quiet again—an awful quiet with the rising sun pale behind slowly rolling clouds of dust. For a moment, silence held the city. Then there was the beginning babble of voices as people, rushing into the streets everywhere, began to speak again. There were excited voices. There were calming voices. There were voices crying out in pain. There were voices calling in fear for loved ones. And there were thin and terrified voices, begging for help from deep within the rubble of smashed buildings.

Enrico Caruso crawled from his bed. He stood trembling in the midst of the chaos that had been his bedroom. Then, according to what is now an old San Francisco legend, he ran to a window and threw it open. He had to learn just one thing; he had to know if he had been terrified right out of his voice. He leaned out over Market Street, and a series of high, clear notes cut through the dusty air. At least, that's the way the story goes.

It was now almost 5:14 A.M.

The earthquake, with its ten-second interval, had lasted between sixty-five and seventy-five seconds.

# Chapter Two

# THE LONG FAULT

1.

EVEN AFTER ALL THESE YEARS, many people all over the world still think that the earthquake of 1906 struck only San Francisco. This is understandable, for the quake triggered a chain of disastrous events that destroyed almost all of an internationally known city.

But the belief is far from the truth. The fact is that the quake knocked down a string of smaller cities, damaged farms and readjusted the scenery for a couple of hundred miles along California's 780-mile length; historians John Castillo Kennedy and Oscar Lewis, respectively, set the length of the affected area at 192 and 210 miles. It ran from Point Arena on the Mendocino County coastline far north of San Francisco to San Juan Bautista in Monterey County, upward of one hundred miles south of the city. Left in its wake was a twenty-to-forty-mile-wide swath of death and destruction.

As frightening as it was and as suddenly as it struck, the quake nevertheless could not have come to a complete surprise to Californians. Ever since man first ventured there, the state has been known as "earthquake country," its first recorded trembler occurring in 1769, when a hard jolt threw the Santa Ana River's channel off course near what is now Los Angeles and frightened the soldiers of Spanish explorer Gaspar de Portola as they were making camp close-by. In memory of the upheaval, Portola christened the Santa Ana "The River of the Sweetest Name of Jesus of the Earthquakes."

Why is California called "earthquake country"? Geologically, its surface consists of great areas of rock which are separated by long and deep breaks, called faults. Due to pressures that build up deep within the earth, these areas push hard against each other along the faults, bending the rocks there out of shape. In time, the strain becomes so great that the earth must snap itself back to its original contours. When it does, it forces the areas on either side of a fault to slip past one another, sometimes horizontally, sometimes vertically and sometimes in a combination of horizontal and vertical movements. At that moment, California has an earthquake on its hands.

In one respect, California can be thankful for its earthquakes. They are responsible for much of the state's magnificent scenery. Over several millions of years, they have collapsed the land to form great valleys and have upthrust it for several thousand feet to create magnificent mountains. The Sierra Nevadas, along with the state's southern mountains and much of its rocky coastline, are the result of earthquakes.

Countless faults are to be found not only in California but throughout the world. Mostly, though, they are concentrated in areas where the earth is still shaping itself. One of the world's greatest collections of faults extends from east to west through Europe and Asia Minor. Another forms what is called the Pacific Basin seismic belt. California is a part of this belt.

Girdling the vast reaches of the Pacific, the belt takes in

New Zealand and the Fiji Islands deep to the southeast and works its way north and east beneath the sea through the New Hebrides, New Guinea and the Philippines to a stretch of the China coast. From China, it travels northwest through the islands of Japan to Russia's Kamchatka Peninsula, touching the southern coast of Korea en route. It next extends across the Bering Sea to the Aleutian Islands and Alaska, curving then to drop along the Canadian coast. After skipping the northwest corner of the United

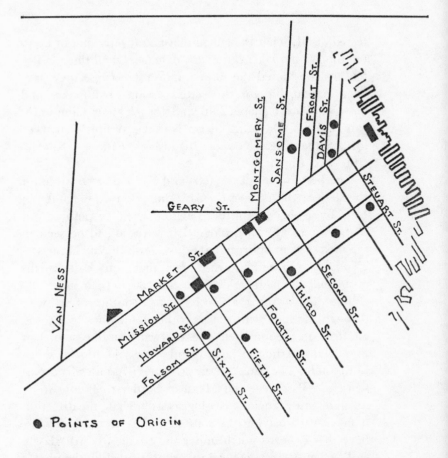

● POINTS OF ORIGIN

States, it runs down through California, Mexico, Central America and the western face of South America. Deep within the belt are the Hawaiian Islands and a northeast-running cluster of small islands immediately west of Guam.

California, in common with all its fellow areas in the Pacific Basin belt, is crisscrossed with hundreds of faults. They are shifting constantly, with most of their movements being so light that they are hardly felt or not de-

tected at all; scientists gauge that about only one in every
ten thousand quakes causes any damage. Of all these faults,
ten are considered the most important because they have
been responsible for the state's major earthquakes and
most significant changes in land form. Their names are:
San Andreas, Hayward, Sierra Nevada, White Wolf, Gar-
lock, Santa Ynez, Newport-Inglewood, Elsinore, San Jacinto and Imperial.

The best known of the ten—and the one responsible for
the 1906 earthquake—is the San Andreas fault, so named in
1895 by geologist Andrew Lawson when he pointed out
that its most typical geological features are to be seen in
the area of San Andreas Lake just south of San Francisco.
The fault is so well known, in fact, that many Californians
mistakenly blame it for every earthquake in their state.

The San Andreas fault runs southeast-northwest
through the state, with several other fault lines branching
off from it, among them the Hayward fault east of San
Francisco and the San Jacinto and Imperial faults far south
in the state. The San Andreas stretches 650 miles from San
Gorgonio Pass near the Mexican border to Point Arena
north of San Francisco. Geologists still debate the direction
it takes after leaving the state at Point Arena. Many believe that it heads north under the Pacific toward Alaska.

The San Andreas is not just a simple break in the earth's
crust. Rather, like all major faults, it is a wide belt containing a network of smaller fault lines within its width.
At certain points, the San Andreas belt—or zone, as it is
often called—is less than a hundred yards wide; in most
places, however, its width stretches from several hundred
yards to upward of a mile. Its exact depth is unknown, but
geologists figure that it slices down into the earth for some
twenty or thirty miles.

Slippage at points along the San Andreas has given California eighteen major earthquakes, along with dozens of minor ones, since men began recording tremblers in the state. Among the biggest of these major upheavels were those that occurred at Tejon Pass on the southern section of the fault on January 9, 1857; at the cities of San Luis Obispo and Hollister along its central section on April 11, 1885, and April 8, 1961, respectively; and at San Juan Bautista along its northern reach for the twenty days between October 11 and 31, 1800.

The other major quakes along the northern stretch of the fault all centered around San Francisco. In June of 1838—the exact day is unknown—a trembler shook the whole San Francisco Peninsula from the city southward; little is known of this quake, for the city and the peninsula were only sparsely settled at the time. Quakes rattled San Francisco and some of its surrounding towns on October 18, 1865, and again on March 22, 1957.

Between these latter, of course, came the 1906 earthquake. It began when the earth to either side of the San Andreas suddenly shifted horizontally along those two hundred or so miles of its length. The shift was so great that the earth to the west side of the fault slipped as much as sixteen feet north of the earth on the opposite side, with the average horizontal movement being ten feet. There was vertical movement, too, causing the ground to either side of the fault to rise from a few inches to four feet in places. It is estimated that the shift was centered between ten and twenty miles below the surface. The harsh trembling—behaving like the ripples created when a stone strikes water—fanned out for twenty to forty miles on all sides of the fault.

It is believed that the fault began its slippage somewhere

under the Pacific a few miles off the northern California coast. The rift moved swiftly toward the land. This was its course as it came ashore and swung south.

NORTH

Assuredly, one of the first men to feel the quake was the captain of the steamer *Arago*. As he was sailing about ninety miles north of Point Arena, his ship lurched violently, as if she had crashed into some sort of object. Reports of the time give differing accounts of the captain's feelings at that moment. One claims that he thought he had struck a log raft. Another says that, though he knew he was in twelve fathoms, he thought that he had gone aground. Perhaps both ideas flashed through his mind as his ship staggered from bow to stern.

Whatever his feelings, he was joined in his confusion by thousands of people in the next seconds. First, a massive cone of masonry broke away from the crown of the Point Arena lighthouse as the splitting fault came ashore. Then the bridge at nearby Alder Creek jerked so violently that a section of it crashed into the creek bed. The western bank moved itself northward, so far northward, in fact, that the bridge was yanked completely off to one side of the roadway that ran up to it.

After that, as the quake traveled south along the fault and sent its rolling waves out in all directions, the destruction came fast. Huge redwood trees toppled near the Gulala River. A quicksilver mine close-by the little town of Guerneville collapsed, trapping and killing three men. At the port city of Fort Bragg, a giant smokestack crashed down among the buildings of the Union Lumber Company mill. A fire broke out and leveled most of the town's business district.

Down into Sonoma County came the quake. The walls of the church that Russian settlers had built at Fort Ross back in the early nineteenth century buckled. Its sloped roof and two wooden towers descended to ground level. The church had to be rebuilt and stands today as a state historical monument.

In Sonoma, the quake rolled out twenty miles from the San Andreas to devastate the quiet little city of Santa Rosa, the home of horticulturist Luther Burbank. The ruin left behind equaled that found anywhere along the disturbed fault. The plant of the *Santa Rosa Press Democrat* caved in, smothering three newspaper boys who were folding that morning's edition; a fourth youngster was dragged from the wreckage by printers. The City Hall roof subsided, and the dome on the County Courthouse crashed through several ceilings before coming to rest on its side on the third floor, where it remained for weeks, looking like a grotesque, sleeping monster.

Even before the earth stopped trembling, fires broke out in the ruins, fires caused by ruptured gas pipes, broken chimneys and overturned lanterns. Fortunately, the Santa Rosa firehouse remained standing, and its two small engines were pulled out and put to work. They were soon joined by a little pumper that raced over from nearby Sebastopol to lend a hand. They battled throughout the day and into the night before extinguishing the flames.

While the fires were being fought, people hurried to the ruined buildings to free their trapped neighbors. From some they lifted the injured, and from others they saw dust-covered people emerge, miraculously unhurt. One man crawled from beneath a pile of charred rubble to say that he had given up all hope of rescue and was waiting for the flames to engulf him when he suddenly felt the wonderful splash of cold water from the little engines. But most of all in the smoking ruins, they found the bodies of dead friends.

Altogether, seventy-five people died at Santa Rosa. Later statistics showed that, of all the California cities lashed by the quake, this little town lost the greatest proportion of its population. Had the same proportion been lost in San Francisco, there would have been a death toll of between eight and ten thousand. Santa Rosans realized that the havoc in their city was caused as much by poor construction as by the violence of the moving earth. Within days, they had their sleeves rolled up and were rebuilding their city into a stronger place, at the same time harboring hundreds of friends and relatives who, not knowing how severely Santa Rosa had been hit, hurried there from devastated San Francisco.

The quake moved into Marin County, immediately north of the Golden Gate, announcing its arrival with a terrible rumbling noise. The two-story hotel at the seaside vacation settlement of Marshall jumped off its foundations and landed in Tomales Bay, a narrow strip of water spearing in from the Pacific. A fisherman out in the bay saw a great wave rise and sweep down on him, tossing his open boat high; he said the wave looked "a mile high" as it pounded toward him; then, when he was calm again, he judged it couldn't have been more than a ten-foot swell. His story later helped to quiet the rumors that a giant tidal wave had hit Tomales Bay and the various beach towns along Marin's Pacific shore.

The quake arrived at Point Reyes Station, overlooking

the Pacific, just as the morning train was being readied for its daily run to Sausalito, where commuters would pick up San Francisco-bound ferryboats. The conductor, who was just climbing aboard, flung himself to the ground and scampered away as the whole train—engine and all—was flipped over on its side. In the same moment, a brick chimney smashed through the station roof. There were no injuries on the train and, oddly enough, not a single window in all its cars was broken.

Something even more remarkable took place at the nearby Skinner dairy ranch at Olema. The San Andreas fault ran directly through the ranch, and what happened there left one of the most striking examples of how far to the north the land on the west side of the fault was moved. The entire geography of the place was changed in seconds. Here is how historians Oscar Lewis and Carroll D. Hall describe the weird occurrence in their book *Bonanza Inn:*

> ... In the barn at Skinners dairy the routine morning milking was going on. The farmhouse stood north of the barn; both structures faced the county road. At the roadside in front of the house stood a row of cypress trees; between the trees and the house was a rose garden. A little beyond the house and farther up the road were a row of eucalyptus trees and some raspberry bushes. Along the east wall of the barn were a number of windows and under each was a pile of manure. The earthquake struck violently, throwing both cows and milkers to the ground and causing the animals to stampede.

All this was bad enough, but, Lewis and Hall continue, when the milkers rushed from the barn, they ...

> ... found that a drastic realignment of landmarks had taken place. The cypress trees and the rose garden had

been moved away from the front of the house and now stood in front of the barn. The clump of raspberry bushes had slid down from the north and occupied the space vacated by the roses. The eucalyptus trees had marched to a position opposite the barn and in the process one had shifted from the foot of the line to the head. The piles of manure before the barn had each moved some sixteen feet south of the window to which it belonged.

Near the Skinner dairy, a terrified cow blundered into a rift left by the shifting fault. At the time there were many rumors of the fault's opening to swallow both humans and animals—remember the man who "saw" all the cattle disappear into Market Street—but this Marin County incident was one of the very few cases where such an occurrence was actually noted. The earth closed in on the animal, trapping her with her hindquarters above ground, and she had to be covered over in a sort of burial where she was.

On rolled the quake to the southern limits of Marin. As the fault broke open beneath hills, great banks of earth gave way, leaving chasms as much as twenty feet wide. In other places, the shifting banks of the fault closed even tighter together than before, except that one side was now up to sixteen feet farther north than the other. At Miller Creek, a short distance from Point Reyes Station, the width of the creek bed was reduced by six feet. The bridge there did not collapse; it simply arched its back six feet at one end.

The quake broke free of the coast at Bolinas Bay, about ten miles north of San Francisco, and followed the splitting fault out to sea for a time. Its rolling movement, however, slammed into San Francisco and fanned out eastward across the Bay to such towns as Oakland, Alameda, Berkeley and Hayward. In the Golden Gate, it caused a tidal action that dropped the water level four feet in ten minutes. Somehow, though, all the violence bypassed the Bay island of Alcatraz and the military prison looming above its rocky shoulders. Not a single brick in the prison buildings came loose, and some people there were not even awakened by the trembler.

EAST

Fortunately for the people of San Francisco, the towns on the east side of the Bay were not seriously damaged by the quake. It was fortunate because these cities—particularly Oakland and Berkeley—were able to house thousands of refugees in the next days and send much aid to the stricken city.

But they did not escape damage altogether. Walls were cracked and chimneys toppled in a series of towns. No deaths were reported in Alameda and Berkeley, but Oakland lost five people when a wall in the Empire Theater collapsed onto the roof of the apartment house next door. The fronts of several stores in the downtown area fell into the streets. On one street, the front of the uppermost story in a building dropped four stories to the pavement; left undisturbed, even with most of their windows unbroken, were the first three stories. Other buildings, among them the First Baptist Church on Telegraph Avenue, though they did not collapse, were so badly shaken that they had to be pulled down later. Fire broke out in one section of Oakland, but it was quickly doused, for the city's water system had gone undamaged.

The quake waves spread out east, north and south from Oakland. They reached as far inland as Stockton, more than fifty miles away. All through the East Bay area, damage was reported as fairly light, restricting itself mostly to smashed crockery, bent doorways and cracked or fallen chimneys.

SOUTH

After heading out to sea at Bolinas Bay in Marin County, the splitting San Andreas turned inland and came ashore at Mussel Beach, a few miles down the San Francisco Peninsula. It went thundering through the Baden marshes at San Bruno and ripped apart the great pipes that carried the city's main water supply to San Francisco from the Pilarcitos, Crystal Springs and San Andreas reservoirs. The reservoirs themselves were left intact; but with their pipes gone, their water was beyond the reach of the city. It was a loss that would be keenly felt in the next days.

About forty miles south of the reservoirs, the quake knocked down almost all of the business district in the little town of Palo Alto. Just outside the town stood fifteen-year-old Stanford University, built by California millionaire Leland Stanford in memory of his son Leland, Jr., who had died of fever in Rome while in his teens. The school, with its large quadrangle and its buildings of sandstone, was one of California's great landmarks, a source of pride to everyone in the state. The quake did its best to level the whole campus. It very nearly succeeded.

The brand new gymnasium caved in, followed by sections of the nearby library. A workman was killed beneath a falling smokestack. A student died when the freshman dormitory, Encino Hall, collapsed. The roof of the great church to one side of the main quadrangle dropped to the floor; the air pressure created by the fall blew out the upper half of the building's front wall.

Facing the quadrangle along with the church was the science building. Ranged along the outside of its second story was a series of statues of famous scientists. One of them, that of American naturalist and teacher Louis Agassiz, toppled from its perch and buried itself to its shoulders in a concrete walkway below, leaving its marble legs thrust straight up in the air. In the next days, according to William Bronson in his book *The Earth Shook, The Sky Burned*, the sight of the statue inspired a number of student and faculty jokes, prompting "quips such as, '. . . the headforemost scientist in the U.S.' and '. . . a fine fellow in the abstract, but no good in the concrete.' "

Though most of its buildings were damaged, the university was far from being destroyed—at least, as far as its spirit was concerned. Stanford president David Starr Jordan, after surveying the ruins, called the quake nothing more than a passing "incident" in the school's history. He said that the school would rebuild itself and become greater than ever before. It was a promise that Stanford kept.

Close to fifteen miles south of Palo Alto, near the sleepy little mission town of Santa Clara, one of the great tragedies of the day occurred. There the Agnews State Insane Asylum suffered the full fury of the quake. John Castillo Kennedy, in his book *The Great Earthquake and Fire*, gives this account of the horror:

> . . . a patient cried, "I'm going to heaven in a chariot of fire! Don't you hear the rumble of the chariot wheels? It's coming to get me!" With a roar louder than chariot wheels the two-block-long building collapsed with many

of the surrounding buildings. The Superintendent and his wife were dead; eleven nurses were dead; eighty-seven patients out of one thousand and eighty were dead. Scores lay pinned, still alive, in the wreckage. A giant inmate, in a momentary flash of sanity, lifted a fallen beam off one of the guards, and then ran off into the hills. It was days before workers dug the last body out of the wreckage, before a dozen deputy sheriffs rounded up the last of the madmen.

Bronson, in *The Earth Shook, The Sky Burned*, adds these notes on the tragedy at Agnews:

... More than a hundred inmates and a dozen keepers died under the falling walls at the time of the quake. Pandemonium broke loose, but although rumors spread through the Bay Area that hundreds of insane were roaming the countryside, no serious incident was ever reported.

Young men and priests from Santa Clara University (about two miles away and itself damaged, though not as badly as Stanford) were among the first to reach the spot. Most of them ran all the way. It was a grisly scene. The mangled bodies of some had already been dragged from the ruins by survivors, and hundreds of the inmates wailed and cried "bloody murder," as one of the young students, now Father Ernest Watson, noted. Some of the more violent patients had to be strapped to trees with sheets and blankets to keep them from harming others. One kept calling, "Jesus of Nazareth is passing."

All during that day and the day following, wagons moved in a steady procession to San Jose carrying the dead and wounded. The final death count: 119.

Agnews stood on the outskirts of San Jose, at one time the capital city of California. Within the city itself, the quake did much damage. It shook the two-story Vendome

Hotel near the downtown district so violently that the whole wooden structure fell over to one side. In the downtown section itself, the Meyer Brothers clothing store caved in, and the brick upper front of the Unique Theater pitched out into the street, falling past the long marquee and leaving it almost unscratched. Fires broke out in two downtown locations. The fire department worked throughout the day to extinguish them. Then a large area around the fires was roped off for a time, and the state militia was assigned to guard it against looters and sightseers.

South out of San Jose went the quake, spreading its waves both east and west. In turn, it hit such towns as Gilroy and Salinas, knocking down the six-story Spreckels sugar mill near the latter. Passing through the Santa Cruz mountains, it bent sections of railroad track four to five feet to one side, caused a landslide on Los Gatos Creek, and smashed two railroad tunnels. At Hinckley's Gulch, it set landslides in motion on both sides of the 100-foot-deep gorge; the slides covered completely the Loma Prieta sawmill on the floor of the gorge; giant redwood trees, as high as the gorge was deep, were moved from their original spot to a place directly over the sawmill and its nine buried workers, as if nature, in a passing flash of gentleness in these moments of its fury, had intended them as gravestones.

Out of the mountains the quake moved. The cities of Hollister, Santa Cruz and Monterey were hit. In the next seconds, it was deep in Monterey County, reaching at last the quiet Pajaro Valley. Here, it shifted the piers of a railroad bridge eighteen inches to the northeast. And, here, it began to lose its strength. It ran on for a couple of miles, smashing the venerable old mission of San Juan Bautista. After that, the San Andreas broke open no more.

But the waves from the quake rolled on, fading with each passing mile, until, with practically all their vitality spent, they reached Los Angeles, where they rattled a few windows.

Finished now was the cataclysm that would affect the lives of several million Californians for days and weeks and months to come, changing the lives of some for all time. The main quake would be followed in the next hours and days by a series of diminishing aftershocks. Most Californians would feel those aftershocks as they dug their dead and wounded from their rubble and got to the job of rebuilding their towns and homes and starting life anew.

But, for San Francisco, those shocks would come in the midst of a new catastrophe, one born of the quake and one that would reap far more damage.

There was fire in the broken city.

# Chapter Three

# THE STUNNED MINUTES

## 1.

BY THE TIME THE EARTH stopped trembling, fires were to be seen everywhere in San Francisco, erupting from any number of sources—broken hot chimney flues and stoves, scattered coals and firewood, overturned kerosene lamps, smashed gas pipes and severed electric lines. Fifty-two were reported to the fire department within a half-hour after the quake, but what the total count must have been is anybody's guess, for there were many, perhaps several hundred, that were quickly stamped, watered or beaten out by alert householders without a word to firemen.

Those fifty-two reported fires were located within and near the downtown district, with firemen bringing several of the latter under control by midmorning. One company fought down a roaring house fire at Buchanan Street and Golden Gate Avenue out beyond Van Ness Avenue. Nearby, other companies knocked out a half-block-long blaze at Octavia and Fulton Streets and a house fire at Hayes and Laguna Streets. All were in neighborhoods of wooden construction.

But the fires right inside the downtown district—these San Francisco's 585 firemen could neither extinguish nor control. There were more than a dozen of them, and they were to turn the city into a hell on earth until the end of the week.

It is perhaps a miracle that the firemen were able to put out as many of those first blazes as they did, for right from the beginning they found themselves up against two almost insurmountable handicaps.

First, the quake left them with no way of receiving alarms and pinpointing fire locations. Their department alarm system, housed in a building in Chinatown, was a shambles; the floor was buried under shattered glass. The system had been operated by a string of wet cells set in glass jars on long shelves, and every jar lay smashed on the floor. Thus, only two crude methods for locating a blaze remained. It had to be pointed out to the firefighters by some distraught citizen, or they had to dash through the streets sniffing the air and searching the skyline for some trace of smoke.

Far more frightening was the second handicap—the lack of water. This handicap was encountered by one fire company after another as they drew up before burning buildings in the first post-quake minutes and ran their hoses out to nearby hydrants. The adventure of the men of 38 Engine Company, as Bronson relates it in *The Earth Shook, The Sky Burned*, illustrates what happened to practically every fireman in the city before the morning was done.

Headquartered north of Market Street, 38 Engine dashed down Market to Steuart Street, which was just a block from the waterfront. There, the firemen discovered flames shooting out of a boardinghouse and spreading to another building. Bronson writes:

> One of the men threaded a hose onto the hydrant across the street and turned the valve. The men who held the hose braced themselves. But there was no rush of water.

The man at the hydrant turned the valve off, then on again, but the torrent never came—just a feeble trickle that soon died away.

They tried the hydrant around the corner on Mission, but the story was the same: nothing but an impotent trickle of muddy water. They tried one more time before the suspicion became a forbidding truth: the water mains were broken, and there would be no stopping the fire here.

The men of 38 Engine—as did every other fireman that morning—diagnosed the situation correctly. The water mains were indeed broken, but the firefighters could not guess just how complete and terrible the breaks were. The pipes leading to the Pilarcitos, the San Andreas and Crystal Springs reservoirs on the Peninsula and to the water supply in Alameda County were so badly sheared and smashed that they would not be even partly repaired until week's end.

To make matters even worse, still another source of water for San Francisco had been put beyond the fire department's reach. Inside the city limits were three great storage tanks, containing upward of eighty million gallons. But the pipes to these tanks, too, had been shattered by the moving earth.

All the water that was left intact for use added up to about 850,000 gallons. Those gallons were stored in the remains of a system of sixty-three underground cisterns that had been built to serve the city back in the days of its infancy, in the days immediately following the Gold Rush. Of the sixty-three cisterns, only twenty-five remained. They were sprinkled throughout the older sections of town.

Nevertheless, it was with these gallons that the firemen

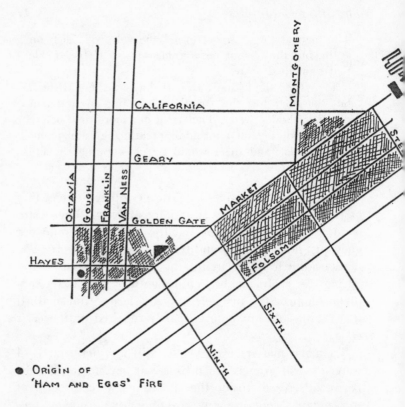

● ORIGIN OF
'HAM AND EGGS' FIRE

performed the miracle of putting out those morning blazes near the downtown section. But, of course, this supply could do little or nothing to stem the tide of those more-than-a-dozen truly big fires that had taken hold in the downtown district.

These major fires all erupted between the harbor on the east and Sixth Street on the west. They divided themselves between the neighborhoods to the north and south of Market, with four to the north and eleven to the south. Those on the north side were centered around the whole-sale and produce districts and on Sansome Street, which was just a block over from the financial district.

These were the fifteen fires that were to wed themselves
into a solid sheet of flame that would sweep through San
Francisco this Wednesday and the next two days and
nights. They would be joined in the next couple of hours
by a blaze that would unexpectedly erupt just west of Van
Ness and then, early in the night, by a fresh fire near
Union Square. Together, they would reap a harvest of destruction that would make the damage wrought by the
earthquake seem tame by comparison.

The quake, registering an intensity of IX on a scale that
measured intensities from a minimum of I to a maximum
of X over at the Unitersity of California's Berkeley
campus, caused widespread havoc, to be sure. But it must
be remembered that, of all the buildings in the city, only
a minority suffered great damage or collapse. Most were
harmed only slightly, particularly those in the western
neighborhoods and those of sound construction. The greatest damage was done in the areas of flimsy building materials and fill earth.

The fires were to pay no attention to the strength or
weakness of any building or to the ground on which it
stood. The city's finest and strongest buildings were to fall
right along with its poorest and oldest places. Before they
were done, they would reduce 28,000 buildings and 497
city blocks to charred ruins and would deprive 225,000
people of their homes. They would leave behind an ap-
proximate $500,000,000 worth of damages.

2.

In the moments immediately following the quake, the firemen were the only ones in the city who seemed to act with
any semblance of order. Everyone else—and rightfully

so—had to pass through moments of confusion, shock and bewilderment. All over San Francisco, people flooded out of their homes. South of Market, they poured into the streets to face chaos and to hear the first calls for help and the first screams of pain from their neighbors buried in the rubble. Immediately, many formed work parties and started to burrow into the wreckage in rescue attempts.

North of Market, the Chinese and Japanese of Chinatown and the Italians, Spaniards and Mexicans of Telegraph Hill ran from their homes to the safety promised by the open space of nearby Portsmouth Square. Within minutes, the square was overflowing with terrified people, and panic broke out there when a heavy aftershock struck the city—a panic that developed into a full-scale but short-lived riot. Others dashed pell-mell down to the harbor, some taking shelter beneath the docks. The cries of injured horses and men echoed through the wholesale district.

In all those parts of the city less severely hit, families gathered together on the sidewalks to survey their broken windows and chimneys and to chatter excitedly with neighbors, often pointing off toward the spirals of smoke starting up in the distance. Most hurried back inside to dress for the day. Some tried to put coffee to boil, but found that their stoves or chimney flues would not work. Others, afraid that their homes were more severely jarred than was apparent, moved their cooking utensils out to the curbs, setting up what would be the first of endless "campsites" in the city. Still others, thinking that the damage was as light elsewhere as in their own neighborhood, harnessed up their buggies or got into their cars and went out to see the "sights," particularly the fires now visible from the downtown district. A young society woman, Elsa Maxwell, had a luncheon date with Enrico Caruso, and she felt the quake would not interfere with it. She went out-side to have a look at her neighborhood, returned to help tidy up her home, and then began to dress for her appoint-ment.

So far as Caruso was concerned, the luncheon appoint-ment was completely forgotten. After testing to see that he had not lost his voice, he grabbed his autographed photo of President Theodore Roosevelt and rushed into the corri-dor outside his room, bumping into other members of the Metropolitan Opera Company. He threw his arms around John Hertz, conductor of the company's orchestra, and shouted that he wanted nothing more to do with San Fran-cisco. Then he turned about, hurried back into his suite and, with the help of his valet, packed all his suitcases. Several minutes later, he was seen sitting in their midst down in the lobby.

After a time, Caruso decided to join other members of the company in viewing the damage outside. They made their way a few blocks west along Market and then turned north, coming at last to Union Square. Here, they en-countered a large crowd that had sought the safety of the open space. About now, Caruso realized that the earth-quake, terrifying as it had been, had not seriously inter-fered with his appetite. He went across Powell Street to the St. Francis Hotel for a breakfast of bacon and eggs, then went back to the Palace to sit on his luggage and clutch his Roosevelt photograph and wait for transportation out of the city.

In the apartment near Van Ness Avenue, the young actor John Barrymore swung himself off the divan and surveyed the room about him. He shook his head sadly. All but one of those valuable pieces of Chinese porcelain that had reached his friend just yesterday from Shanghai now

lay shattered about his feet. He walked to his friend's bedroom and said wryly, "Come look at what's happened to
the crockery." After that, the two men walked into town,
to Union Square.

3.

Though everyone but the firemen seemed to be in helpless
confusion during those first post-quake moments, there
were pinpoints of order here and there, pinpoints that
would grow in the next hours and days into an organized
fight against the fire and an organized effort to keep the
city in good health and spirits until the disaster was a thing
of the past and San Francisco could begin to rebuild herself again.

There was order among the rescue parties that quickly
took shape. Sometimes just one man began tearing away at
the rubble; within minutes, he was joined by others; and
soon thereafter, they formed themselves, sometimes even
without speaking, into loosely knit groups, with the various members taking on particular jobs. Some held back
timbers while others removed the unconscious or dead.
And there was the beginning of order in the wagons and
carriages and trucks and automobiles that were com-
mandeered or that volunteered to remove the injured to
hospitals.

And, very quickly, even before the arrival of the injured
at their doors, there was a growing order at the city's several hospitals. At Emergency Hospital closeby City Hall,
doctors and nurses and patients pulled themselves from
beneath the fallen walls and ceilings, helped by neighbors
who came rushing over to lend a hand. As soon as each was

freed—no matter whether he was doctor, nurse or patient—
he turned to the job of releasing others. The patients were
then hurried across the street to the Mechanics Pavilion, a
giant auditorium and sports arena. Quickly, it became a
temporary hospital. It would continue in that capacity
until the fire roared toward and then over it.

Amidst this growing order were Police Matron Mrs.
Kane and Patrolman John McLean, who had dashed from
beneath the collapsing City Hall only to realize that they
had left six insane patients in the detention ward. Back to
the building the couple went. They made their way to the
frenzied patients and quieted them with comforting words.
Then, leading them out into the dusty sunlight, they
gently tied them together by their wrists and walked them
four miles through the ruined city to the Presidio, the U.S.
Army post that sprawled over the green and wooded hill-
sides above the Golden Gate. Patrolman McLean returned
to the downtown district. Mrs. Kane remained at the Presidio, knowing that she would be needed to attend to the
hundreds of injured that would assuredly arrive there
soon. She did not leave or lie down to rest or change her
clothes for the next three days.

One of the men most responsible for bringing the first
vestiges of order to the city was a fiery forty-year-old Brigadier General, Frederick Funston, the commander of the
U.S. Army's Department of California. He was, this morning, the ranking Army officer in the city by virtue of the
fact that Major General Adolphus Greeley, Chief of the
Pacific Division, was on a visit to Hawaii. After the quake
had flung him from his bed, he checked to see that his wife
Edna was not injured, hurriedly climbed into his uniform,
gulped down a cup of coffee and rushed out in search of

San Francisco's Mayor Eugene Schmitz. He guessed that
the city was badly damaged and that Army troops would
probably be needed to help restore and maintain order.

Funston's home stood on the northern slope of Nob
Hill. He strode up to California Street at the crest of the
hill, looked between the mansions there and knew immediately that indeed troops would be needed. Spread below
him was the entire downtown district. Everywhere, there
were tumbled walls and buildings knocked cockeyed. Off
to the southeast, smoke was starting to billow skyward.
Southwest, the dome of City Hall loomed above naked
girders. The streets were jammed with people, most of
them still in nightdress.

Funston, squat and red-bearded, clamped a cigar between his teeth, lighted it and wondered where he might
find Schmitz. He decided that the Mayor, if he was still
alive, would not be able to occupy his City Hall office;
from here, the place looked too battered for use. He
elected to begin his search at the closest fires—those burning on Sansome Street near the financial district. He
started to walk down the eastern face of Nob Hill, not
wanting to take the time to get his horse, which was sta-
bled several blocks off his course. For all he knew, the
animal might be dead. He hoped he might catch a passing
cable car or hail an automobile.

Of course, no cable cars were operative, and passing
motorists paid him no heed, so he had to walk the whole
distance. All about him, he saw growing evidence of the
quake's wrath. Things looked worse than he had first ima-
gined, and he cursed aloud that he had to waste time
searching out Schmitz. It would be much better to call out
the troops immediately. But the law forbade federal soldiers to enter a city without first being invited by local

authorities. Consequently, he had to go through the motions of placing the troops at Schmitz's disposal and of hearing the Mayor—unless he was six kinds of fool—say that he would be happy to have them.

Through his anger and impatience, impressions of the morning reached Funston. What hit him hardest was the silence. Hundreds of people were in the streets, but the shock of the quake and the devastation had seemingly struck them dumb after their first seconds of babble. He later wrote that there was "not a single sound, no shrieking of whistles, no clanging of bells." Nothing.

He reached Sansome Street and, panting, stared at the burning buildings and the firemen. Most of the firemen, he saw, were standing helplessly about; a few were beating at ground-floor flames with blankets, axes and coats. He heard that the water mains were broken, that there were even worse fires south of Market and that Chief Dennis Sullivan was hurt and perhaps even now dead. He asked for Schmitz, but no one thus far had seen the Mayor. A policeman said that Schmitz might be with Chief of Police Dinan over at the Hall of Justice, a few blocks away. But, on the other hand, he might be elsewhere. He might be anyplace. No one knew.

Funston chewed his cigar angrily for a long moment. Then he reached a decision. He would dally no longer in what might be a fruitless search for the Mayor. He would ignore the law. He would call in the soldiers without invitation and face the consequences, if any, later. He swung about, tried to hail several passing cars, cursed when he failed, and started back up Nob Hill.

The decision to summon the troops on his own responsibility was a dangerous one, he knew, even though there was an apparent need for them. If subsequent events proved that their presence was not really required, then he could be severely criticized and even court-martialed for breaking the law. But he didn't worry much about this possibility. He was accustomed to danger.

To some it seemed that the Ohio-born Funston had lived with danger all his life. He had mined the Yukon for gold, had operated a coffee plantation in Central America and had joined Cuba in her revolt against Spain, a fight that had finally developed into the Spanish-American War in 1898. He had commanded the Cubans' artillery for them, had been shot through one lung and had been captured by the Spanish.

With the Cuban war over, he was made a colonel in the U.S. Army and given command of the 20th Regiment in Kansas. His outfit had been shipped to the Philippine Islands, where he ran into another revolution, this one against the United States, caused when this country took over the Philippines after releasing it from Spain in the Spanish-America War. It was Funston who finally put an end to the revolt by leading his troops through the jungles of Luzon and capturing General Emilio Aquinaldo, the Philippines leader. He had thus been appointed a permanent Brigadier General and had been assigned to San Francisco as commander of the Department of California.

And so it was that he was now striding up Nob Hill. He stamped into the Army stables, stared briefly at the soldiers gathering there and began to snap out orders. To one young soldier: mount up and ride to Fort Mason on the northern shore of the city and bring back every Engineer trooper you can put your hands on. To two officers: ride to the Presidio and march all the troops there into the city. Have engineers and soldiers report to Police Chief Dinan at the Hall of Justice. Minutes later, the riders were on their way.

It was now just after six o'clock in the morning. By seven, the first of about five hundred Fort Mason and Presidio soldiers would come marching down Market Street from the Hall of Justice, to be joined later by sailors, Marines and the California National Guard. They would remain on duty throughout the course of the raging fire, their very presence causing most people to assume that martial law had been declared in San Francisco, when actually this was never the case. Their work would be varied. They would help control crowds. They would arrest looters and shoot a few of them down. They would help fight the fire, and early this Wednesday evening, several of their number would accidentally start one of their own. Some would make hundreds of new friends through their work and their kindness. Some would make just as many enemies. Some would perform courageously and brilliantly. Some would behave stupidly. The next days would show them for what they were—the best and worst of human beings.

With his initial orders out of the way, Funston mounted up and rode to his headquarters down on Market Street for a few minutes. Then he was back in the saddle, where he was to remain for the rest of the day, roaming from one street to another, issuing orders, encouraging his troops to keep on their feet when they were ready to drop in exhaustion and bolstering their spirits by his very red-bearded presence. For years, he had been known affectionately throughout the enlisted ranks as the "Little Man of War" or simply "Freddy." Today, the terms had an extra meaning to them.

At 10:15 A.M., he dismounted to dictate a telegram to Secretary of War William H. Taft in Washington, D.C. In it, he described the disaster and implied that he was using troops without city invitation: "I shall do everything in my power to render assistance and trust the War Department to authorize any action I may have to take. . . ."

To this, he added his first assessment of the number of homeless and his first plea for assistance: "We need tents and rations for 20,000 people."

A soldier took the message and headed through the smoke to the Postal Telegraph Office, which was still in business on Market Street near the Palace Hotel. Funston swung back into the saddle. He glared up at the fiery skyline and chewed hard on his now dead cigar.

He wondered if he had asked for enough tents and rations. He wondered if Mayor Schmitz was alive and unharmed.

# Chapter Four

# DISASTER: NORTH OF MARKET

## 1.

GENERAL FUNSTON need not have worried about Schmitz. The Mayor, though rudely shaken out of bed by the quake, was unhurt, and a few minutes later, even as Funston was hurrying down to Sansome Street, the Mayor was dressed and riding in his carriage to his office at City Hall.

Eugene Schmitz was thirty-eight years old. He was a heavy-set handsome man who sported a neat goatee and a sweeping moustache. There was a mingling of Irish and German blood in him. By profession, he was a violinist. He had at one time directed the orchestra at the Columbia Theater near the Palace Hotel on Market Street. He had been Mayor for five years.

So far as many of his fellow San Franciscans were concerned, he was the worst man ever to hold the job. They never hesitated to say that he and Abe Ruef, the sharp-featured little lawyer who had gotten him elected, had done nothing but fatten their pocketbooks and those of their friends through political graft since the day he had taken office. In the past months, several of the city's richest and most respected citizens had launched a movement to bring him to trial for civic mismanagement. One of them, sugar king Adolf Spreckels, had contributed $130,000 toward the campaign.

Schmitz this April morning was well aware of his unpopularity in many quarters. And he knew there was justice in the campaign against him; he knew there was truth in the talk of money put in his own and Ruef's pockets for the award of city contracts to certain companies; he knew that he and Ruef had larded San Francisco's civic offices with friends and relatives; and he knew that many illegal businesses in the city stayed open because of "protection" money he and Ruef received from their owners. But there was something that he did not yet know as he rode toward City Hall—that the next days were to be the finest in his political life, perhaps in his entire life. They were to be days that would see him, without even giving it a second thought, lay aside all personal ambition and concentrate only on San Francisco's welfare. Greatness was to seek out many people in the aftermath of the quake. Eugene Schmitz was one of them.

Even now, still dazed by all that had happened, he was thinking that the responsibility of restoring order to San Francisco was his. He was thinking of all the reports he must hear of damage and of all the orders he must soon give. He hurried his carriage forward, eager to reach his office.

His first glimpse of City Hall, however, told him that he would do no work there today. The building, which had taken twenty years to build, had been reduced to a shambles in less than a minute. Some rescue workers were lifting a body from the wreckage of the pillars around the front porch. Policemen, nurses and patients were struggling up from the detention hospital in the basement. They froze in horror during a momentary aftershock.

Schmitz decided to move on to the Hall of Justice at Portsmouth Square. He would set up headquarters there—if it were still standing.

During the journey across town to the Hall, which stood at the northern edge of the financial district, Schmitz had ample opportunity to view the destruction that had visited his city. Store and apartment fronts lay across the sidewalks. Splintered glass was everywhere underfoot. Some lampposts were over on their sides. The cobblestone streets were split open in places. Electric lines sagged low. He had to move slowly through hundreds of people clogging each block. Most were still in their nightdress. He heard just a few voices; most people, now that the shock of the quake was wearing off and they were taking their first good look at the chaos around them, seemed too stunned to talk. He stopped while a fire engine, drawn by two fine white horses, charged across his path. He saw a dust-covered policeman help a woman and three children from their apartment building. Smoke was starting to blot out the morning sun. Schmitz knew that he was seeing the worst blow ever struck at San Francisco.

And that was saying a lot. For in its life—a young one yet when compared with places such as London, Madrid, Paris and Moscow—this city had seen more than a fair share of trouble.

It began life as the small village of Yerba Buena, established in 1776 by Captain Juan Bautista de Anza as part of Spain's program of colonizing the New World. It was then no more than a collection of about twenty houses and huts clustered about the Mission of Sorrows, or Mission Dolores, that priests accompanying de Anza had built, but less than a century later, it erupted into a boomtown.

Causing the eruption was the 1848 discovery of gold in

California. Yerba Buena, with its name now changed to
San Francisco, became the gateway to the gold fields for
the hundreds and then the thousands who hurried westward. Almost overnight, the sleepy little village became a
sprawling tent city. Then up went wooden hotels, boardinghouses, restaurants, saloons, theaters, gambling dens
and stores—all the accommodations needed and wanted by
gold-hungry, adventuring men. San Francisco emerged as a
quickly and carelessly built place, and seemed to have arms
outstretched for trouble.

And trouble arrived, five times within a year, in the
shape of fire. The entire downtown section was burned
down on Christmas Eve, 1849, to the tune of more than a
million dollars in damages. Quickly, starting even before
all the flames had been doused, the city rebuilt herself,
only to burn down once more on May 4, 1850. Rebuilding
got under way again. And then down in ashes everything
went again, in June and September of the year.

Schmitz knew that, ever since then, San Francisco had
lived under the constant threat of fire. It had come to be
called "the most combustible city in the world" by several
fire department officers and more than one fire insurance
company. Behind this reputation were two factors—weather
and the fact that so much of it was yet built of wood.

So far as the weather was concerned, most outsiders
looked on San Francisco as a cold and rainy place. As did
all San Franciscans, Schmitz knew that the idea of much
rain here was nonsense. The city could turn chill and
foggy at the drop of a hat and, when it so chose, the rain
could come down in buckets; but the truth of the matter
was that rain did not fall on her for eight or nine months
out of any year, making her many wood structures as dry
and dangerous as a tinder box. Adding to the danger were

the almost-constant winds from the Pacific. They could fan the slightest blaze into ferocious, spreading life.

As for the heavy percentage of wooden structures in the city, Schmitz knew that there was good reason for them. This was earthquake country, and it was gospel to every veteran resident that, when the earth started to rattle around, wood had a greater resistance to falling down than did brick, that other most popular construction material of the nineteenth century and this dawning twentieth century. You just had to look at the piles of brick now in the street to know the truth of that.

Schmitz had to admit, though, that much of the city had been built foolishly. But the same could be said of any town that had mushroomed in the swiftly growing America of the century just closed.

By the time the Gold Rush had died down back in the mid-1850's, San Francisco was established as an infant city with the potential of growing into one of the most important seaports in the Western Hemisphere. People had looked on it now, not as "the gateway to the gold fields," but as the gateway to trade with Asia. Many gold seekers, seeing the commercial possibilities offered by the city (or just plainly loving the place), had decided to settle here rather than return home. They were joined during the next fifty years by thousands from all over the United States and the rest of the world, until the population this Wednesday was just fifty thousand shy of the half-million mark.

To meet this influx, builders had hammered up every possible kind of structure. Many had done their work without any regard for the lurking dangers of earthquake and fire, just as many lumbermen, much to the current wrath of President Theodore Roosevelt, had denuded the nation's forests without any thought of replanting them. Many local builders had used shoddy materials, interested only in turning a fast dollar and not caring about the lasting quality of their products. Many had worked too fast in trying to meet the ever blossoming demand for stores, offices, restaurants and housing. Many, wanting to put every inch of available space to use, had thoughtlessly filled in hollows and gulches and stream beds and had set their buildings on this most dangerous of all ground in earthquake country.

But, Schmitz told himself, no one could say that all San Francisco builders were slipshod and irresponsible. The more recently constructed neighborhoods out west of Van Ness were sturdily put together. And, through the years, there had been a growing tendency to construct fireproof and earthquake-proof buildings in the downtown district. Prime examples were the Palace, St. Francis and Fairmont Hotels, the *Call* Building and the Montgomery Building, nicknamed the "Monkey Block," over in the financial district. They were signs that the city was beginning to grow up into a responsible lady.

Now, Schmitz thought, the day of testing and of truth was at hand. Many of the city's shoddiest buildings were already down, and it might not be long before everyone saw just how combustible wood really was. And, if the fire got out of hand—and, from the look of the ballooning smoke, it was doing just that right now—San Franciscans would see if, as was claimed, their finest buildings were actually fireproof.

For a moment, sitting hunched over the reins, he wished that he was not the mayor of a fire- and earthquake-prone city. How could anyone live in a place that was rattled around with frightening regularity? For the same reason, he knew, that people remained in tornado and hurricane and flood areas. You were born there, or you loved the place, or you were used to its dangers. And, anyway, earthquakes did not come along as frequently as those other upheavals of nature.

San Francisco's most serious quakes, he recalled, had been recorded in 1857, 1865, 1868 and 1890, with the one in 1868 causing a number of fires. The city's most recent trembler had hit on a Sunday morning last December.

Schmitz grinned suddenly, remembering something about it. It had done little or no damage, but it had been stinging sharp and it had given San Franciscans a story that, as far as Schmitz could see, they had not yet tired of telling. It seems that Father F. P. Driscoll of St. Dominic's Church had been preaching a sermon that Sunday on the Last Judgment, and the quake had come along at exactly the right moment to help him punctuate a point. It had struck just as he was saying, "He shall not come unannounced. Signs shall precede His coming, great signs and fearful—"

The *Call*, reporting on the coincidence, had called it "a remarkable one."

Schmitz remembered smiling when he had read the *Call*'s report. He looked up at the ruined buildings and the billowing smoke. There was nothing to smile about this morning. This was bad, as bad as it could get.

Schmitz arrived at the Hall of Justice and climbed from his carriage to be greeted by Chief of Police Dinan and three police commissioners. The Hall was still standing, but Dinan said that its ground and upper floors were not safe. Its central tower had been knocked loose and another shake might well bring it down. Schmitz nevertheless decided to risk the use of the basement as his temporary

headquarters. He led the Chief and commissioners along
the ground-floor hallway and went down a flight of stairs.
He heard the terrified shouts of prisoners from elsewhere
in the building, demanding to be released.

The basement, with its electricity knocked out, was as
black as night. The men found some candles, lighted them,
set them on a desk and seated themselves in the pale glow.
They were joined by several other men—a sprinkling of
police officers, businessman J. Downey Harvey and Abe
Reuf, the lawyer responsible for Schmitz's election as
mayor.

There was a few minutes of talk as Schmitz probed toward an understanding of the first steps he must take on
behalf of the stricken city. Dinan told him that many off-
duty policemen were already reporting for work, some to
their stations, some to the Hall of Justice, some to points
along the streets where they saw they were needed. The
commissioners estimated that several thousand people
must be already homeless and that thousands more would
suffer the same fate as the fires raged on. There would be,
the commissioners prophesied, looting, and there might
well be an epidemic of typhus or some other disease.
Harvey said that the water system was smashed and that
the firemen were battling the flames with water from the
city's old cisterns and that some were simply hitting at the
flames with blankets.

Schmitz heard them all through. Then he took his first
official action to restore some semblance of order to the
city. He wrote out a short proclamation and instructed
that it be printed in some shop not knocked down by the
quake and then distributed throughout the town. The
proclamation ordered that every saloon in the city be
closed until further notice.

That done, he scribbled out two messages. He sent them off with a policeman to the Postal Telegraph office on Market Street, hoping that it was still standing and that its lines were still open to the outside world.

The first of the messages was addressed to the Mayor of Oakland. It was short and to the point:

"MAYOR MOTT, OAKLAND: SEND FIRE ENGINES, HOSE, ALSO DYNAMITE IMMEDIATELY."

The second message went to California's Governor Pardee. It thumbnailed the city's plight and asked all available relief supplies, from medicine to food, be sent to the city as quickly as possible.

Both messages went out that morning from the Market Street telegraph office. Both received instant response. Oakland dispatched some of her firemen and equipment and then welcomed thousands of quake and fire victims in the next days.

Governor Pardee, as soon as he received Schmitz's message, sent a dramatic wire of his own to Los Angeles:

"FOR GOD'S SAKE, RUSH ALL AVAILABLE COOKED FOOD TO SAN FRANCISCO AS SOON AS POSSIBLE. I WILL SEE THAT THE TRAINS ARE RUSHED THROUGH."

Los Angeles, in its turn, reacted with lightning speed. It loaded doctors and nurses and several tons of medical supplies aboard a special train. The train pulled into burning San Francisco before midnight.

With the proclamation written and the messages dispatched, there was nothing more that Schmitz could do until he viewed the havoc outside. He moved toward the staircase, but businessman Harvey stopped him, saying that he had a suggestion. Harvey recalled the dangers mentioned by the commissioners, the dangers of illness and starvation posed by the city's thousands of homeless people. He suggested that a committee of leading citizens be formed to supervise the details of their health and welfare.

Schmitz nodded and smiled. It was an ironic smile, for he knew full well that practically every man who must be chosen for such a committee would be one who either hated or held him in contempt. Among them, undoubtedly, would be men who were part of the current movement to bring him to trial and thrust him from office.

Nevertheless, at this moment San Francisco was all that counted in his mind. He returned to the table and, with Harvey at his elbow, drew up a list of eighty names, all of them belonging to San Francisco's wealthiest and most influential men. He told a policeman to find the men and inform them that they were being asked to join a "Committee of Safety." They were to meet here at the Hall at one o'clock this afternoon. Harvey took a last look at the list. He smiled. Abe Ruef's name was not on it.

It was now about nine o'clock in the morning. Schmitz walked out of the Hall of Justice to view the fires.


2.


The fires burning closest to him, of course, were those that had started in the produce and retail districts and on Sansome Street. They were burning fiercely and were out of control, with the firemen trying to beat them down with water from the old underground cisterns, with blankets and even with filth pumped up from the sewers. But, compared with the growing holocaust South of the Slot, they seemed to be proceeding in an almost stately manner. South of the Slot, the flames were literally racing through one building after another, feeding hungrily on the old and collapsed wood. But here, north of Market, many of the buildings were supposedly fireproof, made of stronger stuff—of brick and mortar and steel girders and metal window frames. And so the flames did not give the appearance of uncontrollable movement. Rather, they seemed to take a building at a time. While one burned, the tremendous heat seeped into its neighbor. The heat mounted steadily until it could no longer be withstood. Then, dirty gray-black smoke suddenly crashed through windows and newborn flames poured out behind it. Usually, because of the rising heat, each building first took fire in its upper stories.

The fires north of Market were by now burning in three directions—south toward Market, north toward Telegraph Hill, and west toward the financial district along Montgomery Street. In their westward march, they had already burned past Sansome Street and were just half a block off Montgomery.

The fact that the fires were moving at a stately pace meant nothing to the people who worked in the financial district and who had hurried there soon after the quake. They saw the flames above the rooftops a half block over, and their eyes watered with the smoke pouring along Montgomery. In the care of these people—stockbrokers and bankers—were millions of dollars in currency, bonds and stocks. At all costs, these valuables must be removed from the path of the fire.

Charles Crocker, head of the Crocker-Woolworth Bank, had his workers load sacks of money and securities into crates and pitch them into the backs of wagons. He drove the wagons down through the wandering, dazed crowds on Market Street to the harbor. He sought out Thomas Crowley, who ran a string of motor launches on the Bay. He hired one of Crowley's launches, had the boxes stowed aboard and sent the boat out into the middle of the Bay, telling Crowley to leave it there until further notice.

Another banker was not quite so fortunate as Crocker. Into a wagon he dumped a half-million dollars in currency, only to realize that he had no place to take it. And so he hauled it up the street to a more distant bank and put in it the vaults there. Later, he had to move it again.

Another bank, the Anglo-California, poured close to a million dollars in negotiable bonds into two wheelbarrows. Two clerks pushed the barrows down to the Ferry Building. There, they joined thousands of people trying to force their way into the building. They finally managed to board a ferry and got safely away to Oakland.

Amadeo P. Giannini owned the small Bank of Italy at Montgomery and Columbus Avenue, still several blocks north of the closest fires. He lived about seventeen miles south of the city, in the small town of San Mateo. Immediately on being awakened by the quake, he departed for the city to see what damage, if any, had been done to his little bank. He found that the commuter train was not operating, and so he walked into San Francisco, a journey of five hours. He reached his destination just after noontime, found the bank unharmed and heard his clerks say that the fires would never come this far north. He went out for a brief look at the blazing skyline, deciding immediately that he disagreed with the clerks. He obtained two wagons and had all the bank's funds loaded into them. Late in the afternoon, he took the wagons to the apartment of an employee. Then, after a makeshift dinner, he and two clerks drove south to his San Mateo home, where they secreted the money behind his living room fireplace.

Several days later, Giannini was back in San Francisco and had opened two small branch banks for his customers —one in the financial district, the other out on Van Ness. Some weeks later, he settled in new quarters. From there, his bank grew into the largest in the world, en route changing its name to the Bank of America.

Bankers, however, were not the only ones busy that morning in the financial district. Joining them in their furious activity were officials of the magnificent Sutro Library, which was housed in the Montgomery Building at Montgomery and Merchant Streets. The library had been assembled by tycoon Adolph Sutro, who had made millions in his Comstock silver mines. It contained upward of 200,000 volumes, among which were priceless Gutenburg Bibles and Shakespeare folios. The officials gathered wagons outside the great brick building and, after frenziedly emptying the library contents into them, hurried through town to the Mechanics Pavilion, a giant auditorium and sports arena just across the street from the ruined City Hall.

They unloaded the crates and placed them in a corner of the Pavilion, which was now being used as a hospital and which was jammed with more than three hundred injured people from the streets, from Central Emergency Hospital and from City Hall's detention hospital. In time, the library move proved to be a poor one. Somehow, the brick and concrete Montgomery Building survived the financial district fires, while the Pavilion burned to the ground long before the day was done.

3.

While all this furious activity was in progress, a young
Army lieutenant was leading a half-dozen or so artillery
caissons into the financial district. The caissons were
loaded with barrels of black powder that the Army had
collected from its ordnance stores at the Presidio in answer
to an appeal from Assistant Chief John Dougherty, who
had taken command of the fire department on learning of
Chief Sullivan's injury. Back at the Presidio, more barrels
of the powder were being piled aboard wagons. The stuff
was to be used to blow up buildings in the path of the
flames, thus creating firebreaks.

Briggs, the young lieutenant, did not like at all the idea
of using the black powder. He knew that Dougherty had
called for it in desperation; the Chief would never have
asked for it had the city's water supply been available. But
Briggs also knew that the powder might do more harm
than good. It was temperamental stuff and might very well
blow up in the untrained hands of firemen. It always went
off with a great fiery flash; in a crowded downtown area, it
could then start new fires as easily as create firebreaks.
Briggs wished that he had the authority to forbid its use.

He brought the caissons through the financial district
and halted them at Sansome Street. Squinting and shield-
ing his eyes with a cupped hand, he stared up at the towering flames and felt their heat scorch his face. The air was
thick with choking smoke. The sun had disappeared behind rolling gray-black clouds. Blackened firemen and
Dougherty assembled about the wagons. The firemen had
been fighting a useless battle, pouring what little water was
available on the flames and beating at them with blankets,
sacks and clothing, but Briggs immediately saw that they

did not greet the black powder enthusiastically. They eyed it warily, knowing as well as he that it could be more enemy than useful tool.

And so he quickly put into words a thought that had entered his mind as his caravan had rumbled through the financial district. There was, he said, stick dynamite over at Angel Island, north across the Bay, near Marin County on the opposite side of the Golden Gate. It was much safer to handle; so why not send for it and store the black powder somewhere until its use was absolutely necessary? The firemen agreed quickly. A messenger was dispatched for Angel Island. Briggs sighed with relief and moved the caissons up Montgomery to the comparative safety of Portsmouth Square across from the Hall of Justice. A few minutes later, the wagons bearing the rest of the powder from the Presidio rumbled into sight and were halted.

The Angel Island dynamite did not arrive at Sansome Street until just after noontime. Now on the scene with Briggs were Mayor Schmitz and the police commissioners. Shocked, the lieutenant heard Schmitz and commissioners decide to use the dynamite on buildings adjacent or close to structures already afire. He intervened quickly and angrily. What was being proposed, he said, was equally as dangerous as the use of the black powder. The dynamite should be set at more distant points and the blasted areas then cleared as much as possible before the arrival of the flames; only in this way could firebreaks work successfully. If nearby buildings were blown up, their debris would only add fuel for the fire.

Schmitz and the commissioners understood his logic. But they could not agree with him. They argued that they were responsible for the structures in the city. They, not Briggs, had to answer to angry owners and the general public if they ordered distant blocks to be destroyed, only to find in a few hours or days that the fires were not destined to reach that far. No, they would have to gamble on the nearby buildings. They ordered Briggs to send half the dynamite supply to the firefighters south of Market and then to begin the blasting here on the north.

The young lieutenant had no choice but to shrug and obey. Nature had triggered the fires, he knew. Now, he told himself, tired and frightened men were going to help them along.

# Chapter Five

# DISASTER: SOUTH AND WEST

## 1.

THERE WAS NO HESITANCY about using the dynamite south of Market. The firemen, soldiers and volunteer workers there welcomed it. They were so desperate that they were ready to try anything, no matter how dangerous, to halt the fires raging round them.

"Raging" actually is too tame a word to describe the temper of the Wednesday holocaust South of the Slot. Within an hour after the quake, those fires that had started out down near the harbor joined hands and turned themselves into a solid wall of flame. It literally raced west and north through the endless rows of poor wooden buildings; it leaped from street to street, flashing by above the heads of bewildered firemen; it devoured whole blocks at a time and sent its fiery sparks swirling on ahead to set new fires that it then soon overtook. As early as 9:00 A.M., its northward arm reached sections of Market and, just a short distance down from the produce district, met a branch of the Sansome Street fire to turn one stretch of Market into a flaming tunnel. By noontime, just as the dynamite was arriving, the southern fire had devastated the eleven blocks west from Steuart Street to Sixth Street and the three long blocks between Market on the north and Folsom Street on

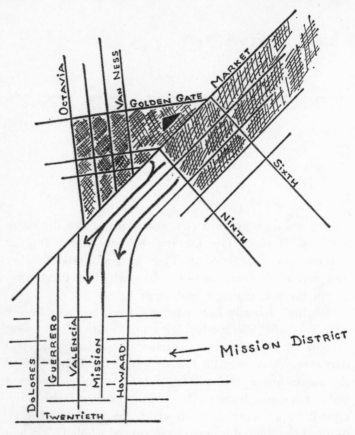

the south. Miraculously, firefighters thus far had kept the flames from jumping Folsom to roam farther south.

To make matters worse, the south-of-Market firefighters early in the day were faced with an unexpected danger from the northwest. Over beyond wide Van Ness Avenue, in a crowded residential district known as Hayes Valley, a housewife went back into her apartment shortly after the quake and decided to cook a breakfast of ham and eggs for her family. She did not stop to think that her chimney flue might be broken; at least, she didn't give it a thought until

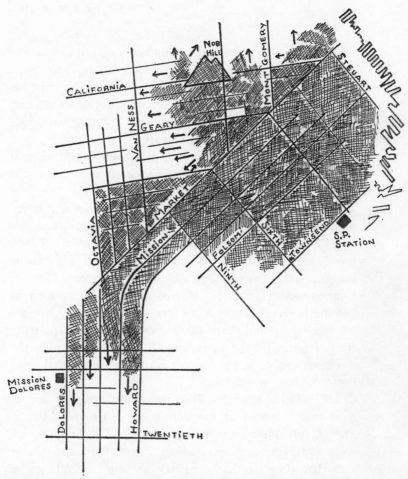

she had lighted her wood stove. But then it was too late.
Sparks escaped the flue and immediately set the apartment
building ablaze. From there, the fire spread to the rest of
the block and then roared east and southeast—east toward
Van Ness and the City Hall just beyond, south toward
Market. Before the morning was done, it was christened
the "Ham and Eggs" fire.

The firefighters south of Market had only to glance northwest and see the rolling smoke to realize that a new danger was fast approaching. They knew that, if the Ham and Eggs fire jumped Market, they would be caught between two solid walls of flame. Little wonder that they grabbed eagerly at the arriving dynamite and began laying charges along Eighth Street to create a firebreak there.

As desperate as the situation was south of Market, it must be said that not every square inch of the burning area was afire that Wednesday morning. For instance, the stretch of harbor just one block over east from devastated Steuart Street remained untouched, thanks mainly to two small boats that were sent down from the Mare Island naval base on the northern reaches of the Bay. One was the tugboat *Active*; the other, the fireboat *Leslie*. Marines jumped ashore from the *Active* and joined firemen in beating back the flames from Steuart. The *Leslie* chugged relentlessly up and down the harbor all day long, pouring tons of water on the piers. In this manner, not only the southern harbor but the Ferry Building were saved from destruction.

Also saved was the San Francisco Mint, a huge square of steel and concrete at the corner of Fifth and Mission Streets, just one block south of Market. The firemen, soldiers and Mint employees who gathered there thought at first that they would have little trouble defending the place against the fire; its thick walls and metal window frames would surely withstand any attack. But the fire had other ideas. It reached the buildings opposite, and its terrible heat reached out to shatter the Mint's windows and melt their frames. The men inside found themselves running in all directions at once. They poured water from a basement cistern on all the woodwork that ignited with every crashing window. They toted buckets up to the roof to wet down its smoldering tar paper surface. Then they rushed back inside to save their lives when the fire roared past. Finally, back onto the roof they went, to stamp out every small blaze left behind. In all, it took them seven hours to put out all the fires that erupted in the building. Their efforts saved an estimated $40,000,000 to $200,000,-000 in bullion and coin locked in the Mint's vaults.

Spared, too, was the great gray Post Office building two blocks to the west, at Seventh and Mission. Inside, postal employees used mail sacks soaked in water to beat out dozens of small fires ignited by the intense heat. Outside, in the early afternoon, firemen and soldiers fashioned a firebreak around the place by dynamiting a series of modest frame houses. As soon as the Post Office was deemed safe, its employees got busy handling the tons of mail that went out of San Francisco in the next days to worried friends and relatives everywhere.

But these buildings were just a fortunate few, a scant few. All about them, the destruction was complete. The Army Medical Supply Depot on Mission went early, taking with it much equipment that could have been put to good use throughout the city. Soon after, the Opera House, close-by the mint, was in flames; in little more than an hour, the scene of Caruso's triumph of the night before lay in ashes. St. Patrick's Church burned to a shell, the red glow playing over its steeple, which the quake had hurled to the street.

The southern fire worked itself up to Market along Third Street, moving into the shops and offices behind the *Call* and *Examiner* Buildings and the Palace. Among the first Market Street structures to go was the eighteen-story *Call* Building. Its death struggle began when the heat got

inside and mounted slowly with growing intensity from
floor to floor until, at the fourth story, the windows suddenly shattered and fire burst out through them. The draft
thus created turned the building into a giant flue, and the
heat swept up to the dome and exploded into flame. After
that, the fire methodically worked its way, a floor at a time,
back to the ground, leaving behind a blackened shell.

All along the south side of Market to Sixth, other landmarks fell to the fire—the squat *Examiner* Building; the
Emporium department store, with the State Supreme
Court on its top floor; and the California Academy of Sciences headquarters. Only the Palace Hotel remained untouched on this stretch of Market by noontime, its great
bulk looming haughtily above the flames, its flag atop a tall
staff appearing now and again in the smoke. But it would
not last much longer. Its time would come at two o'clock.

As if the fires were not bad enough, Market Street all
morning long was choked with thousands of people. There
were, first, all the people fleeing their smashed and burning homes to the south. Whatever few precious belongings
they had salvaged, they now carried on their backs or
pushed along in wheelbarrows or baby buggies. There was
a woman dragging a sewing machine. There was a family
struggling with an upright piano. There was a woman
holding a bird cage with its floor missing and its occupant
gone. There was a father shouting for his wife and children. There was a woman wandering about with a dead
infant in her arms and pleading with passers-by to tell her
that the baby was alive and well and that the falling beam
hadn't really hurt it after all. There was a man with a half-
dozen hats stacked one inside the other atop his head.
There were children, all of them dazed and frightened,
some of them clutching toys or loaves of bread or little

bundles of clothes, and some of them forgetting the horror of the day long enough to laugh at the man with all the hats. All these people were moving north and west and east—north and west to parks and squares, east to the Ferry Building for boats out of the city.

And there were the firemen and the soldiers and the policemen. The firemen raced from building to building, in attempts to head off approaching fires, to snuff out new blazes, to clear threatened buildings of rescue workers. They used any weapon they could find to battle the holocaust. They emptied cisterns on it. They splashed it with wine and whiskey. They pumped sewage up through their hoses. They seemed to be everywhere. They crowded about empty hydrants and cursed them. They stared up, angry with helplessness, at each new burning building. They were on the seventh floor in the *Call* Building when the windows three stories below shattered and the place went afire. They ran for their lives.

Close-by always were the soldiers and policemen. They pushed and guided the fleeing hordes along their way. They held the crowds back from the fires. They carried away the injured. They scattered thieves reaching through the display windows in stores. Once, a soldier yelled at a man who was bending over an unconscious woman and who seemed to be plucking at the rings on her fingers. The man jumped up and tried to run away. A single rifle shot felled him.

And, finally, there were all the people from the western neighborhoods who, not realizing the seriousness of the fires, had come downtown in their buggies and cars to see the sights. Horrified, they found themselves caught in the shove and push of the fleeing thousands. Some drivers immediately swung about and ran for home. Others had not

the room to turn and were trapped. Some climbed down to
help with the fires and rescue work. Some took the fleeing
refugees aboard and began moving out to safety. Others
knocked aside outstretched and pleading arms. General
Funston appeared, reining in his horse alongside some soldiers. He loomed above the crowd as he yelled to the soldiers and pointed at the cars and buggies. Immediately, the
soldiers moved forward and began to take them over as
ambulances.

Pushing against the tide of fleeing refugees right along
with the cars and buggies was forty-seven-year-old Alice
Eastwood. She was not, however, coming downtown on a
sight-seeing tour. Her destination was the California Academy of Sciences headquarters, located midway along the
south side of Market between Fourth and Fifth. She was
Curator of Botany there, and she was determined to rescue
her nationally praised botanical collection from the sixth
floor. She arrived at the Academy shortly before it went
afire. She sighted an attorney of her acquaintance and led
him inside. They climbed along the iron railing left behind when the quake had knocked down the central stair-
way, reached their destination and packaged as many
plants as possible and lowered them to the ground floor.
Miss Eastwood then hurried out into the crowded street,
where she managed to hire a wagon to take her bundles
to a friend's house on Russian Hill. Later, she carried
them out to Fort Mason along the Bay shore at the northern tip of Van Ness, putting them at last beyond the reach
of the fires. Her work of that day ranked among the finest
done in her sixty years with the Academy.

While Miss Eastwood was climbing through the ruined
Academy, there was bedlam down at the Ferry Building.
Within minutes after the quake, hundreds of people de-

scended on the structure that had been built in 1898 and that could handle 50,000,000 passengers a year. The first arrivals found the gates locked, and they raged against them, demanding to be put aboard ferries bound for Oakland or any other town across the Bay. When the gates were finally opened, there was a blind rush to the piers. Adults and children were trampled underfoot. It was one of the rare instances of outright panic on that day and those that followed. Some semblance of order was restored with the arrival of police and soldiers. Cordons were set up and all incoming people made to stand in lines to board the ferries that were soon shuttling endlessly back and forth across the Bay. Thousands of refugees flocked into the place before day's end. Outside, the tiny *Leslie* prowled the edge of the Bay, spewing water on the building and the adjoining piers.

Far over to the west, the Ham and Eggs fire was pressing in on Van Ness near Market by eleven in the morning. Already it had destroyed hundreds of homes and apartments and the Slavonian Church. Now, still a few blocks ahead of the fire, the massive St. Ignatius Church on Van Ness felt its heat. The heat mounted steadily and became intolerable, and the spires of what was considered the finest Jesuit church in the world exploded in flame. Next the body of the church went and, with it, priceless murals and a giant pipe organ. Then the flames were across Van Ness and eating toward City Hall.

At Mechanics Pavilion across the way, exhausted doctors and nurses, many of them cut and bruised, watched in horror as the flames approached. The Pavilion was doomed, they knew. Hours earlier, after digging themselves out of the ruins of Emergency Hospital and the detention hospital wing at City Hall, they had scoured the rubble and had moved all their patients over here, placing them on makeshift litters and on mattresses dragged out of the hospital. Within minutes, they had been surrounded by the first of the injured pulled from nearby smashed buildings, then by all the bleeding and broken-boned who dazedly wandered in under their own power and then by all the maimed and torn brought in by car and buggy and wagon from more distant points. Operating tables were set up. Dead bodies were placed in one corner. The Sutro Library officials had pushed through a side door and stacked their precious books along one wall.

Now there was thick smoke rolling through the cavern-like building. The air turned stifling. Glowing, wind-blown cinders landed on the roof and burst into tiny flames. In a minute, the whole roof was afire. Far below, the place was alive with movement. Nurses grabbed children and ran for the main door and then struggled back for more. Doctors, volunteer workers and the walking injured hurried stretchers outside. Bandaged men, women and children staggered or, if they could not stand, dragged themselves over the floor to the exits. The Sutro officials threw their books back into their wagons. The sound of voices shouting orders or calling for help or crying out in pain was deafening. Cars laden with the injured roared away. Buggies and wagons clattered after them. In fifteen minutes, the building had disappeared behind a swirling mass of flame. To this day, no one knows for certain if anyone was left behind in the doomed Pavilion. Rumors of the time said that three hundred people died there. Later and calmer assessments held that practically everyone—if not every last person—escaped to safety.

The Ham and Eggs fire reached Van Ness and the burning St. Ignatius Church. It turned south toward Market. The firemen south of Market saw it coming and grabbed at the arriving dynamite.

## 2.

The firemen set their first dynamite charges along the east side of Eighth Street, two blocks away from the wall of flame advancing from the harbor. Teams of soldiers and volunteer workers ran ahead of them, clearing the last residents from their porches, charging through buildings and hammering down doors to see if anyone remained within. Some people left meekly, dazedly. Others protested; they couldn't believe that their homes were doomed; they argued that they had no place to go. These the soldiers roughly shoved into the street and prodded off with bayonets. Then a voice rang out, "All clear!" The fireman backed to the far side of the street. A series of dull explosions split the air. One wooden building after another seemed to expand from within itself and then fell in a heap.

The firefighters moved east, right up to the oncoming flames to dynamite any buildings that the fire had somehow overlooked. Had the young Lieutenant Briggs seen them now, he might have felt a thrust of grim satisfaction, for it was immediately evident that the dynamite was going to do more harm than good. The wreckage of the buildings now detonated simply provided better fuel for the fire, and it raced on even faster than before. On top of this, the dynamite took its toll in human life. A young Army officer ran into a store to see why a charge had failed to explode; it blew up in his face. In a Mission Street

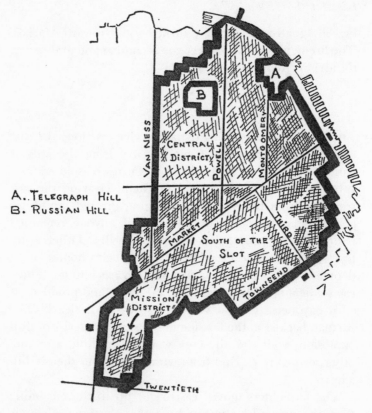

A. TELEGRAPH HILL
B. RUSSIAN HILL

VAN NESS

CENTRAL DISTRICT

POWELL

MONTGOMERY

MARKET

SOUTH OF THE SLOT

THIRD

TOWNSEND

MISSION DISTRICT

TWENTIETH

flophouse, soldiers could not move three drunken and terrified men. The soldiers at last shrugged and fled for their own lives, leaving the three to die when the building came down in a heap moments later. Only in one spot did the dynamite prove beneficial. It cleared those small buildings around the Post Office, thus creating an effective firebreak and insuring the safety of the great structure.

The fire rushed on to Eighth Street and ate swiftly into the dynamited rubble there. The heat began to peel the paint from the buildings across the way. Soon they were smoldering, on the verge of exploding into flame.

General Funston reined to a halt on Market. He listened to the sound of the detonations from both the north and south. They were coming so fast that he thought they sounded like an artillery barrage. To the northwest, he saw the Ham and Eggs fire crawling toward Market. It was obvious now that it would come out on Market at about Ninth. If it then jumped Market, it would be a block away from the southern fire. They wouldn't waste any time joining hands to swing down beyond the South of the Slot region to the crowded residential area called the Mission District.

Funston pulled out his watch and glared at it. His hands left black smudges on its face, and he saw that it read just past two in the afternoon. Without looking up, he knew that, with the exception of the firefighters, policemen and soldiers, Market Street was now pretty well deserted. All the fleeing crowds of this morning had disappeared—to distant parks and squares, to the Ferry Building far down the street beyond the rolling smoke or to the Southern Pacific Railroad station over to the southeast at Third and Townsend Streets, just beyond the present lower boundary of the southern fire. All this was good. At least, the men fighting the fires had working room. And, at least, since many of the refugees were no longer on the move, some sort of aid could be brought to them. He recalled his telegram to Washington and its plea for tents and rations for twenty thousand people, and he wondered if it had yet reached its destination.

The little General put his watch away. He looked southwest, sighting only smoke and fire, but seeing in his mind's eye the cramped streets of the Mission District. Undoubtedly most, if not all, of their householders would still be there, having no place else to go and feeling that

the flames were still too far away to be of real danger. But
once the fire reached them, they would be on the move,
adding thousands to the number already homeless. He
shook his head. It didn't matter whether his first telegram
had reached Washington. It was now sadly out-of-date.

He kicked his horse and raced along Market to the first
soldier he sighted. He leaned down from the saddle, dic-
tated a new telegram for Washington, and ordered the soldier to take it across the Bay to Oakland for dispatch if the
Postal Telegraph office down Market was not still in business. The soldier saluted and trotted away, the back of his
uniform coat black with perspiration from the shoulders to
the waist.

The telegram in his hand read:

"We need thousands of tents and all rations that can be
sent. Business portion of city destroyed and about 100,000
homeless. Fire still raging. Troops all on duty assisting
police. Loss of life probably 1000. Best part of resident
district not yet burned."

Funston's mind ran over that last line as he watched the
soldier move off. He wondered how long it would hold
true.

# Chapter Six

## THE YELLOW AFTERNOON

1.

ALL THROUGH THE MORNING, the great Palace Hotel had remained aloof to the surrounding flames, and there were those gathered on the street at New Montgomery and Market who, right from the beginning, had said that she was just too massive and fireproof to fall prey to any disaster. Inside, her employees had seemed to agree; the quake had rattled her teeth, that was all; now the fire would assuredly do no more than scorch her hide. And so they had acted accordingly, and their behavior in the first post-quake hours had been in sharp contrast to the frenzied activity found elsewhere.

They had moved with deliberate calm and dignity, as if this day were no different from any other, even as they hurriedly dragged hoses along her corridors and through her eight hundred rooms, wetting down overheated walls, window frames and drapes with water from basement and roof cisterns. They spoke courteously and quietly, no matter whether they were storing delicate lamps and linens in relative coolness of the basement or carrying luggage down to the lobby for those guests determined to get out of San Francisco as fast as possible. In the high-ceilinged dining room, white-jacketed waiters served breakfast to the

*89*

more imperturbable guests. They paid little attention to
the yellow smoke that poured in from the streets as they set
plates of bacon and eggs in place. Hardly an eyebrow was
raised when the burning rear wall of the *Examiner* Building just up Market fell in with a crash that echoed through
the entire hotel.

If there was any fear in the employees, it was for the
welfare of friends and loved ones outside, and this, because
they were well trained in their work, they kept hidden so
as not to alarm further any of their already distraught
guests. For their own skins, they had as yet little real con-
cern. They knew what many of the firefighters out on the
street knew: that millionaire banker William C. Ralston
had built the place back in 1868 with earthquakes and fires
in mind. Its foundations were twelve feet thick. Its brick
walls were reinforced with steel and concrete. There was
water on the premises, about three quarters of a million
gallons, in a vast basement cistern and seven roof tanks. As
far as they could see, if you had to be in San Francisco this
day, you might as well be in the Palace.

The lobby was the only place in the building where fear
was out in the open. Here, hastily packed luggage was
piled high. Here, frightened guests sat or stood huddled
together and watched the morning's horror out on Market
and New Montgomery, and gasped at the thunder of the
first dynamite explosions, and died a little at every report
and rumor of the spreading fires. Assisted by harried clerks
and bellboys, they bargained and begged with draymen
and carriage drivers to haul them and their luggage somewhere to safety. Enrico Caruso sat in the midst of his suitcases, his autographed photo of Teddy Roosevelt still
clutched to his chest, and cursed San Francisco as an " 'ell
of a place" and told anyone who would listen that he

would trade it any day for Vesuvius in his native Italy and that, if he got out alive, he was never coming back.

Actually, Caruso was among the first to leave the hotel. Sometime about midday, the Metropolitan Opera Company managed to hire a wagon for its players. Caruso climbed in with the rest and rode away to spend that night somewhere out in San Francisco's western region.

By 1:00 P.M., the downtown fires were on all sides of the Palace, and there was real worry among the employees now as they rushed here and there with firemen, soaking down rooms and flooding the roof, all in an unflagging effort to drown the dozens of small blazes set by falling sparks. Most of the guests had been evacuated and the rest were leaving now. The heat was stifling. Everyone was choking and gagging in the smoke clogging every corridor and room. The water in the basement and roof cisterns was running low, much of it having been drained off for use on nearby buildings. It seemed impossible, but it looked as though the five-million-dollar structure was not going to survive. The flames outside, unless they miraculously turned away or subsided, were going to prove too much for it. Bartenders began to hand out bottles of some of the most expensive liquors to departing guests and workers.

Out in the street, firemen and policemen and soldiers kept looking anxiously at the roof. For most of the time, what they were trying to see was hidden in smoke, but every once in a while the yellow-black clouds parted and they could see it—the hotel's flag flying from its slender mast. Somehow, in their minds, it had become linked with the building's survival; so long as it flew and was visible, if only now and again, the Palace was not yet engulfed in flames. They could not know it, but they were not alone in their feeling. From hilltops and slopes all over the area north of Market, thousands of eyes were strained for a glimpse of the flag.

Then there were hoarse cries running along New Montgomery out to Market. Fire was in the rear of the hotel. Now it was in the corridors, now in the rooms, now in the kitchens. The last of the firemen and employees dashed from the building. Above their heads, windows shattered and filthy black smoke poured out over Market and New Montgomery, followed almost instantly by swirling flames. The fire spread over the roof, and the smoke there grew black with burning tar paper. The firefighters fell back from a solid wall of heat.

It was just after three o'clock in the afternoon. For an instant, a cleft appeared in the mountains of smoke. There was a cry from everyone who happened to be looking at the roof at that moment. The flag was gone.

2.

When flames at last gripped the Palace Hotel, their heat spread out across Market Street and caused another place that had become a landmark that day to be abandoned. It was the Postal Telegraph office.

The small office put in a heroic nine hours until its doors were closed at 2:30 P.M. Like its competitor, Western Union, its wires were damaged by the quake, but whereas Western Union was unable to get back into operation, the Postal Telegraph operator managed to have a line open to the outside about thirty minutes after the quake. Until midafternoon, it was to be San Francisco's single thread of communication with the rest of the world.

Over it, to anyone who might be listening, the operator clicked out the first news of the disaster. He is known today only by the initial "R" with which he signed the message. It read:

"There was an earthquake hit us at 5:15 o'clock this morning, wrecking several buildings and wrecking our offices. They are carting dead from the falling buildings. Fire all over town. There is no water and we lost our power...."

"R" was apparently a man who did not lose his sense of humor even in the midst of catastrophe, for he added:

"I'm going to get out of the office as we have had a little shake every few minutes and it's me for the simple life."

The message is marked with a 5:50 A.M. time signal. It is not known whether "R" had a change of heart about leaving or was replaced by another operator. Whoever manned the little office must have been a very busy man indeed, for it was soon besieged by hundreds of people, all wanting to tell distant relatives and friends that they were alive and unharmed. On top of these came official messages. Through all the clamor, the operator also managed to click out word of the progress of the fires—fires that steadily bore in on him from both the north and south sides of Market until the Palace burst into flames and the heat and smoke became unbearable.

At that point, this message went out from San Francisco:

The city practically ruined by fire. It's within half block of us in same block. The Call Building is burned out entirely, the Examiner Building just fell in a heap. Fire all around in every direction and way out in residence district. Destruction by earthquake something frightful. The City Hall dome stripped and only the framework standing. The St. Ignatius Church and College are burned to the ground. The Emporium is gone, entire building, also the old Flood Building. Lots of new build-

ings just recently finished are completely destroyed.
They are blowing standing buildings that are in the path
of flames up with dynamite. No water. It's awful. There
is no communication anywhere and the entire phone
system is busted. I want to get out of here or be blown up.
                            Chief Operator Postal Telegraph Office
                                    San Francisco, Cal. 2:20 P.M.

It was the last word to come from within San Francisco
for the next days.


3.


At 1:00 P.M., about an hour before the Palace started to
burn, the men whom Mayor Schmitz had invited to join
the Committee of Safety began to arrive at the Hall of
Justice. Eighty had been invited, but the group that assembled in the candlelit basement consisted of only twenty-
five. There were several who, in the turmoil of the day,
had not received their invitations. There were others who
could not attend because of injury in their families or because they were busy saving what business records they
could from the path of the flames. There were still others
who, at this moment, were watching helplessly as their
properties went up in flames. And, Schmitz realized with a
wry smile, there were those who were not on hand because
they wanted nothing to do with him.

But the men present constituted the cream of San Francisco's social and economic life. There was M. H. de
Young, the owner of the *Chronicle*; his newspaper plant,
all eleven stories, stood across Market from the burning
*Call* and *Examiner* Buildings and somehow had thus far
withstood the surrounding flames. There was F. B. Strat-
ton, the collector of the port; attorney Garrett McEnerny;

and former city attorney Franklin Lane. And, surprisingly, there were James Phelan and Rudolph Spreckels. Schmitz had expected neither to appear. Both men—the former a previous mayor of San Francisco and the latter a million-aire businessman—were in the forefront of the move to bring him to trial for graft.

Schmitz opened the meeting with a terse but thorough description of the progress of the fires, moving on then to speak of the disease and starvation that must threaten any city where there is no water, where there are ruins and thousands homeless. The men listened silently, their eyes narrowing as he went along, and it is possible that they immediately saw that here was a different Schmitz from the Mayor they had known and scorned. Here was a wrinkled, sweat-stained man who had spent the last hours tour-ing the burning streets and who had come back with but one thought—the city must be brought through this disaster in the best manner possible. There was unsuspected steel in him, and they nodded quickly when he said that he wanted their committee to take charge of caring for the welfare of every homeless San Franciscan—man, woman and child.

For a moment, Schmitz talked of another matter. He said that he was worried about rumors of looting in the burned and ruined blocks of the downtown district. He announced that the soldiers and police had been ordered to shoot thieves on sight and that he understood three had already been gunned down. Then back he went to his con-cern for the homeless. How could they be helped through the coming night? What initial steps could be taken for their safety? What advice could they be given? Suggestions for citizen information came from several directions in the candlelit room: don't light fires indoors; don't wander about the streets; don't expect the return of gas and electric power for some days to come.

On the basis of the suggestions, Schmitz leaned forward and penned his second proclamation of the day:

PROCLAMATION BY THE MAYOR

The Federal Troops, the members of the Regular Police Force and all Special Police Officers have been authorized by me to KILL any and all persons found engaged in Looting or in the Commission of Any Other Crime.

I have directed all the Gas and Electric Lighting Co.'s not to turn on Gas or Electricity until I order them to do so. You may therefore expect the city to remain in darkness for an indefinite time.

I request all citizens to remain at home from darkness until daylight until order is restored.

I WARN all Citizens of the danger of fire from Damaged or Destroyed Chimneys, Broken or Leaking Gas Pipes or Fixtures, or any like cause.

E. E. Schmitz, Mayor

*Dated, April 18, 1906.*

Schmitz read the proclamation aloud, saw the men nod and instructed that five thousand copies of it be made at any operative print shop before nightfall. By sunset, soldiers were nailing them on doors and utility poles throughout every unburned section of the city.

Schmitz now turned his attention to the work he planned for the Committee of Safety. He proposed that the committee be broken down into groups, each to handle specific problems and needs as they arose, and that one committeeman be given the power to sign checks to help the homeless buy food and other necessities. He nodded with satisfaction when the men pledged themselves to make the checks good in case the city treasury ran out of

Smoke from the burning city moves some two miles into the sky. This photograph was taken at 2:30, Wednesday afternoon, April 18.

A general view of burning San Francisco, April 18, 1906.

San Francisco's homeless on the move to the safety of parks and squares on the morning of the quake.

The San Francisco City Hall pictured in ruins shortly after the earthquake. The building had been constructed at a cost of $6,000,000 and had required twenty years to complete. It was destroyed in a matter of seconds in the quake, with fire later eating into it to destroy all city records. Charges of shoddy construction there were heard on all sides after the quake.

This sample of the damage done by the earthquake was taken little less than a month after April 18. The location is Howard Street near Nineteenth, just beyond the limits of the fire that burned its way through the Mission District to the south-west of the downtown area.

Soldiers and police patrol burning Market Street. The tall structure is the Call Building. Farther down the street, the flag atop the Palace Hotel can be seen. The flag disappeared in smoke when the great hotel finally burned. Note the pile of brick on the sidewalk and, in the foreground, the desks and tables removed from an office after the quake.

Workers engaged in the reconstruction of San Francisco take a meal in one of the many public kitchens established throughout the city in the days and weeks following the quake and fire.

Taken almost two weeks after the quake and fire, this photograph shows one of the tent camps set up in parks and squares throughout San Francisco for the homeless —this one in DuBois Park beyond the burned district.

funds. Then, smiling slightly, he heard them appoint Phelan to be in charge of signing the checks. He knew that, as Mayor, he should have got the job himself, but he knew just as well that most of the committeemen would rather hand a civic checkbook to the Devil than to him.

At this point, a policeman hurried into the basement to say that the men would have to leave. The Sansome Street fires had been steadily marching northward through the day, spreading over to the financial district, and were now approaching the Hall of Justice. In a matter of minutes, it was likely to be afire. The time was just a little after three o'clock. Schmitz and the men hurried up to Portsmouth Square. There, they agreed to meet again tomorrow. But where? Schmitz looked toward Nob Hill where the squat bulk of the Fairmont Hotel loomed against the yellow-gray sky. They would meet there, he said. The men nodded and then left.

4.

Lieutenant Briggs was a very disgusted man at a few minutes after two o'clock in the afternoon. For more than an hour now, he and his helpers had methodically blown up a string of little buildings next door to the financial district, his heart wrenching with every explosion. He knew that he was wasting his time. The fires chewed hotter than ever into the remains of every detonated place. The ruins, with their scattered and torn wood and their exposed furnishings, were simply giving the flames a more efficient fuel.

Now a messenger ran up with news that, north of them, the fire had moved into a new block. It was now threatening the Subtreasury Building. If flames got into that building, they would be just two short blocks away from the

Hall of Justice, which had become the headquarters for
the city government. The messenger said that Briggs was
to bring his dynamite north on the double.

The lieutenant and his men hurried up to the first
building on the Hall of Justice side of the Subtreasury
Building. Again, as his men set their charges in the building, Briggs realized with pain that they were wasting their
time. The Subtreasury was doomed, he told himself—and
so was the Hall of Justice. No puny firebreak could keep
the inferno from it.

The roar of the explosion shook the thick air. Windows
flew from the building and spattered over the street. The
structure itself disappeared in a rolling cloud of dust,
smoke and flying mortar and lumber. Then, while the
smoke was still rising, the roof subsided and settled on the
rubble of what had been the building.

Now Briggs faced a new problem. He had used the last
of his dynamite on the building. All that remained was the
black powder stored in Portsmouth Square. Briggs told the
police commissioners on the scene that the black powder
must not be used. Spurting flame as it did when it exploded, it would set more fires than it would stop. The
commissioners shook their heads stubbornly. If the black
powder was all that remained, then it had to be used.
Wearily, angrily, Briggs sent wagons to fetch the stuff here
and to wherever else it was needed south of Market.

The first building chosen to be destroyed by the black
powder was a drugstore at the corner of Clay and Kearney
Streets, a block west of Montgomery and just across from
the southeastern edge of Portsmouth Square. As the men
were setting the charge, Briggs glanced westward up sloping Clay Street. Just a short distance away lay the many
blocks of Chinatown, with its population of Chinese and

Japanese. It was a sprawling neighborhood of narrow streets, a colorful place, with the edges of its many homes and shops and apartments and business buildings fancily trimmed like pagodas and their fronts painted in the vivid colors so dear to the Oriental heart. But, despite their color and charm, they were mostly made of wood. They would burn frenziedly if the fire reached them. Briggs hoped the area could be spared. But that would take a miracle. And this didn't seem to be a day of miracles.

His men came up to say that the charge was set and that the drugstore and the apartment above had been cleared of all occupants. Briggs nodded and waved the signal to get on with the job. An explosion tore the building apart. Briggs closed his eyes in agony, for he glimpsed bits of flaming bedding from the upper floor fly across Kearney Street. The burning stuff landed atop apartments there. They were immediately afire, and the horrified lieutenant saw the flames start their march toward Chinatown. By midevening, its hundreds of brightly painted buildings would be lost in a mass of swirling fire.

Close-by Briggs, the fire raged round the Subtreasury and sent red fangs licking out toward Portsmouth Square and the Hall of Justice. The square itself seethed with movement. Mayor Schmitz and his Committee of Safety were driving or walking away after their agreement to meet tomorrow at the Fairmont. Men were still loading black powder aboard wagons for distribution wherever needed. The last of the refugees who had sought the protection offered by whatever open space remained in the square were fleeing, most of them on foot, dragging their pitiful possessions behind. Several men were placing in wagons the bodies of the dead that had been placed in the square earlier in the day. By five o'clock, the place was almost deserted. Smoke rolled in over it as the fires pressed close to the Hall of Justice. The building would explode in flame shortly after sundown—a sundown that would be hidden behind the yellow-black clouds looming all over downtown San Francisco.

5.

Up on Nob Hill, at the corner of California and Powell Streets, Mayor Schmitz reined his carriage to a halt and jumped wearily down to the cobbled roadway. The intersection—in fact, the entire hilltop—was jammed with refugees, who stood in total silence, watching the fires spread out below them.

For a moment, Schmitz could not bring himself to look at the fires. He was tired, more tired than he had ever been in all his life. He needed a moment to rest. His knees felt weak and ready to buckle. He leaned against the carriage and put a hand across his eyes.

But, even for that moment, there was no rest. All the events of the day kept rushing in on him. He snapped his eyes open and straightened up. There was no use in recalling memories of the day. They only got in the way of thoughts about all the work and decision that lay ahead. Schmitz made himself look at the fires, turning slowly from one front to another.

There, down the hill to the east, the flames from Sansome Street had eaten through the financial district and were moving west in what seemed to be an almost straight line. Their northern edge was right alongside Portsmouth Square and the Hall of Justice, and their southern rim was advancing along Market. Their central section was headed for Chinatown and, just beyond it, Powell Street. Behind the line, and barely visible to Schmitz, lay one block after another of burned-out smoking ruins.

Over to the south, there was a continuous line of fire along the far side of Market all the way west from Steuart Street by the harbor to Ninth Street, a line broken only now and again by blackened shells where the flames had eaten their fill and died out or where, somehow, they had spared a building. Behind Market, the South of the Slot area was burned out south to Folsom.

Finally, over to the west, the Ham and Eggs fire was crawling up to City Hall; it would be inside the place shortly after dark. The fire's southern arm was across Market at Ninth and was joined with the southern fire; together, they were now on their way southwest into the crowded Mission District. The central section was moving toward Powell Street and was now about six blocks distant.

Schmitz turned to the north. Here, thank God, there were no flames. Russian Hill and Telegraph Hill and all the streets between, streets that ran up to the northern rim of the city, were still safe. But if the fires were not stopped ... well, who could guess what would happen then.

Schmitz turned back to look down Powell Street. It fell south, wide and straight, to Market Street, en route passing Union Square on the left and the St. Francis Hotel on the right. The blocks to either side of it were yet to be touched by the fires coming from the east and west, and the section was the only part of the downtown district that bore any semblance of San Francisco as it had been before twelve minutes past five o'clock this morning. But Schmitz could see firemen and their little engines coming into Powell down by Union Square, and he knew why they were there. Acting Fire Chief Dougherty had told him about an hour ago.

The firemen were gathering on Powell Street to make a major stand against the line of fire coming in from the east. It was moving far more quickly than the Ham and Eggs fire and would, they figured, be up to Powell by mid-evening. At all costs, it must be stopped there and kept from sweeping on to meet its companion to the west.

Schmitz climbed wearily back into his carriage. He wondered what chance they had to stop the fire. Perhaps good; the street was wide—that was a main reason for making the stand—and night was coming to the city and might bring its customary damp fog or even rain. More likely, the chance was slim. The eastern fire, as did all the others, seemed to have the fury of a demon in it; the firemen were exhausted, and their little engines pathetic against the massive wall of flame and useless without water.

He rode slowly away through the silent crowds.

What chance?

Night would tell.

# Chapter Seven

## THE RED NIGHT

**1.**

WIDTH WAS NOT THE ONLY REASON for the decision to make a stand along Powell Street. Firemen saw other advantages, three in all.

To begin, there was the great open expanse of Union Square on its east side between Post and Geary Streets right at the base of Nob Hill. It stretched a long block over to Stockton Street, and the firemen thought that it would give them at least one very effective firebreak.

Secondly—and this advantage was intimately linked with the first—the massive St. Francis Hotel stood directly across Powell from Union Square. Though the firefighters had seen some of the city's finest and strongest buildings go up in smoke this day, they felt that the St. Francis had a more than even chance of withstanding the approaching holocaust, particularly since Union Square could hold the flames a block distant from the hotel's front wall. If the St. Francis did manage to survive, then it would add to the effectiveness of the firebreak formed by the Square.

Finally, there were vacant lots sprinkled all along both sides of Powell right up to the crest of Nob Hill. They, too, would serve as firebreaks.

And so the firemen strung their thin hoses out along the

wide street as darkness fell. They hooked them into whatever underground cisterns were at hand or into sewer
lines. Alongside their engines they piled blankets and
shovels and pickaxes, along with any other firefighting
equipment to be found. Soldiers, sailors, Marines and policemen moved quickly through the buildings to either
side of the street, clearing them of their remaining occupants, who then trudged off to the west or, if they wished
to watch the approaching fire, up to the top of Nob Hill.
As each man finished his work, he slumped down on the
curb or alongside an engine to rest and await the moment
when the flames were close enough to begin the job of
wetting down threatened buildings.

Oddly enough, exhausted as they were and beaten on all
sides throughout the day, the men felt a stirring of hope,
the quiet certainty that the flames would not get past
Powell. Perhaps they shared Schmitz's thought that the
coolness of the night, with its traditional possibility of fog,
or even rain, might help their cause. Perhaps they felt that
now they could put up a genuine and effective fight because, for the first time this April 18, they had been given
the chance to marshal their forces properly. Perhaps they
thought that there had been just too much havoc and that
it had to stop soon. . . .

A group of tired soldiers entered the battered Delmonico Restaurant, which stood on O'Farrell Street, just
east of Powell and a block south of Union Square. They
planned either a makeshift dinner or a cup of coffee—no
one knows for certain which they had in mind—and they
lighted a small fire. Somehow, it got out of hand. It set the
restaurant ablaze and leaped to the adjoining Alcazar
Theater. After that, it raced north, south and west.

Running north, it ignited every building on Geary

along the southern border of Union Square. Then it jumped into the streets on the eastern side of the Square and headed toward the wall of flame coming in from the financial district, at the same time charging north in front of it toward Chinatown.

Its southward course carried it down to Market Street, where it multiplied the fires there. And its westward run took it immediately to Powell. It paused for a moment, its red flames shooting out over the heads of stunned and angry firemen, and then it sent glowing sparks flying over to Gunst's Store on the west side of the street. From Gunst's, it moved toward the north-of-Market arm of the Ham and Eggs fire, scattering hundreds of refugees and threatened homeowners.

The firemen could only stand and watch it go, some crying in their frustration and others cursing and shaking their fists at it. Their tiny equipment and thin streams of water were helpless against its fury. The night had just begun and already they had lost a stretch of Powell. What chance would they have when the wall of flame from the financial district was ranged along the whole length of the street?

The Delmonico fire was just one of several misfortunes to hit the city in the early hours of Wednesday night. One struck over to the east, in the midst of the smoking ruins next door to the financial district. Flames, for some unknown reason, broke out afresh there and leveled a block that had miraculously escaped destruction throughout the day. This new outbreak almost cost a couple of dozen people their lives.

They were tenants of the modest Brooklyn Hotel. Just after sunset, they returned to the hotel, which was located just a block distant from Montgomery, and congratulated

themselves on their good fortune when they saw it standing safe along with such neighboring structures as the
Mills and Telephone Buildings. Now they wouldn't have
to sleep the night in the streets. Their rooms were still
thick with smoke. The air in them was stifling, and their
walls were hot to the touch. But they were unburned and
habitable. The people entered them gratefully, some
dropping fully clothed into bed and falling asleep immediately.

Minutes later, there were screams as fire mysteriously
burst afresh among the ruins outside. As if possessed by
some sort of demon, the newborn flames crashed into the
unburned block and headed straight for the hotel. Franti-
cally, the residents grabbed up whatever belongings were
within arm's reach and ran for their lives. As they fled, the
hotel exploded in an angry red glare. Almost immediately,
every other building in the block was afire.

Down through the ruins the flames sped to Market
Street. Standing there amidst the charred rubble were such
as-yet-unburned structures as M. H. de Young's *Chronicle*
newspaper building, the Flood Building and the Columbia
Theater, where Mayor Schmitz had once conducted the
orchestra.

The *Chronicle* Building loomed directly across Market
from the blackened *Call* Building and the caved-in *Examiner* Building. Constructed of steel and granite, it had
withstood the furnace heat of the day, but now flying
sparks settled on its tar-paper roof and blossomed into a
half-dozen or so small fires. The fires grew, joined hands
and crawled down inside the eighth story where all the
linotype machines stood. The flames ate over the floor,
withering the supporting timbers until they could no
longer support the weight of the machines. With a series of

deafening crashes, the linotypes hurtled down through floor after floor to the basement, carrying desks, chairs, filing cabinets and banks of print with them. Behind this grotesque waterfall came the fire, blasting out the windows in each successive floor and chewing at the building's interior until the whole place was nothing more than a ruined shell.

Soon after the *Chronicle* Building went, the flames were in the Flood Building and Columbia Theater, destroying both.

Blocks to the north, another landmark died at about the same time as the *Chronicle* Building. The fires roaring around the now-deserted Portsmouth Square at last got into the Hall of Justice. The tottering old building blazed like a torch for several hours. All the while, the fires from the financial district and Delmonico's Restaurant swept relentlessly toward Chinatown.

In 1906, approximately 25,000 Orientals—Chinese and Japanese—lived in Chinatown, the first of their number having come to San Francisco back in the Gold Rush days. Those first arrivals had been just as eager as all the thousands of incoming Americans and Europeans to "strike it rich" in the gold fields. But they soon realized that they were not cut out for mining, and so they had turned to other pursuits. They settled in the city to open gambling parlors, souvenir shops, grocery stores, laundries, hotels and restaurants or to hire themselves out as cooks and servants. As did so many national groups in every major American city, they built their own community in San Francisco, fashioning it into a miniature Orient of narrow streets, gaily painted buildings and beflowered, but sagging, balconies.

The community grew as thousands more Chinese traveled to California in the next years. The greatest influx came in the 1860's, the decade that saw the Union Pacific and Central Pacific companies, laboring toward each other from opposite directions, build America's first transcontinental railroad. The Chinese went to work for the Central Pacific, laying track inland from the West Coast. On May 10, 1869, the Central Pacific tracks reached Promontory Point, Utah, and joined those of the Union Pacific coming in from the east.

Many of the workers settled in San Francisco's Chinatown, and by the turn of the century, Chinatown ranked as one of the most unusual sections, if not unique, in San Francisco. It was a colorful place full of sharp contrast. Its people ranged from several of the city's wealthiest and most astute businessmen to some of the most poverty-stricken souls to be found anywhere, with the latter often living in tiny airless basement caverns, several families to a room. Lining the streets were places that no tourist wanted to miss, restaurants, souvenir and herb shops, and grocery stores with dried fish and fowl in their windows; beneath them were supposed to be miles of tunnels leading to various opium dens. On the sidewalks could be seen, all at the same time, well-dressed families and some of the worst elements in the city's criminal life—thieves, opium dealers and professional killers.

All these contrasting features were lost in a mass of flame by midevening Wednesday. The fire swept through the district as though its wooden buildings were just so much kindling, which in truth they were. Thousands of Orientals surged along the streets and scattered to all sections of the city, taking with them only those possessions which they could carry on their backs. Hundreds more, perhaps several thousand, failed to escape their homes or basement caverns before the roaring flames crashed down on them.

By midnight, the entire area lay devastated. Its inhabitants returned in the next days to begin the job of rebuilding it into the sturdy and picturesque section that it is today. And, in those next days, San Franciscans learned that the place, as bad as it had been in many ways, had not really been quite as wicked as originally thought. All those tunnels to opium dens—a favorite rumor through the years —had not actually existed. Oh, there had been the opium dens, all right, and there had been some sort of tunnels. But mostly they were just small rooms, built for brief glimpses by tourists who hired guides to show them the "truly dangerous sights" in Chinatown.

With Chinatown now out of its way, the wall of flame hurried on to Powell. As it approached, firemen climbed tiredly to their feet and began hosing down the buildings on the east side of the street. They worked automatically now, with no real hope of success; all they could recall was the ease with which the Delmonico fire had jumped west across their heads. Yet they did not slacken their efforts, particularly those at the job of whipping up and down the long handles that sent water or sewage pumping through the little engines and into the hoses. Whenever one of them collapsed in exhaustion, another stepped in immediately to take his place. Above them, many of the refugees on Nob Hill began to flee westward.

The fire reached Powell after midnight, arriving first at the Bush Street intersection, just two blocks uphill from Union Square. It quickly devoured the wooden shops, hotels and apartments there. Its flames roared so furiously that the streams of water aimed at them evaporated long before they hit their mark. The firemen cursed the night. There was San Francisco's usual wind to help the flames along, but there was no fog and there was no rain.

At three o'clock in the morning, a frightened and disgusted yell went up from the firemen. Sparks blowing overhead had set a church on the west side of the street afire. Hoses were swung about and brought to bear on the frame building. But they were of no use. The church flared like an ignited box of matches and the flames leaped into an adjoining apartment house and began to sweep westward in the residential area that extended over to Van Ness Avenue.

The exhausted firemen continued to play their pathetic streams of water on the towering flames. But they knew they were fighting a lost cause. The fire was across Powell at two points; they could not expect to hold it elsewhere along the street. They heard their officers direct the soldiers and Marines and sailors and policemen to clear the refugees and residents from the streets to the west. Then all the little engines were ordered up to the crest of Nob Hill. It was there that the fire officers saw the next great danger. As far as they were concerned, the neighborhoods over to Van Ness were lost, but if the westward-running fire sent a section of itself up over Nob Hill, then the whole northern section of central San Francisco lay exposed to devastation.

2.

South of Market, the situation was equally desperate. All the blocks between Steuart and Ninth, on the east and west, and Market and Folsom, on the north and south, were smoking ruins, with just a fortunate few buildings, such as the Post Office and Mint, still standing intact. A great torch—the result of the marriage of the Ham and Eggs and southern fires—was moving relentlessly southwest into the Mission District. Teams of firemen were running ahead of it, detonating buildings with whatever stock of black powder remained and sprinkling it with sewage and cistern water.

For a time, the only hopeful thing that could be said about the south-of-Market conflagration was that it had been kept from jumping Folsom Street along its southern boundary. But, early in the evening, even that victory was snatched away. Flames leaped across Folsom and roared south and east all at the same time, burning back toward the harbor along a block-wide front between Folsom and Harrison Streets. The fire was stopped three blocks short of the harbor, but at Third Street it penetrated beyond Harrison and ran down to Townsend, swinging west again to Eighth Street.

At Third and Townsend, the fire raged up to the Southern Pacific Railroad Station and the sheds and yards sprawled around it. Unlike any other night of the year, the station was almost deserted, several thousand refugees having learned early in the day that the quake had halted all railroad traffic and that it was a waste of time to think of escaping San Francisco from the station. The only people on hand were a couple of dozen firemen and sailors. Working desperately and without rest from the time the fire approached at 10:00 P.M. Wednesday night until it died down at about 4:00 A.M., they saved the place from destruction.

That they managed to do so seems little short of a miracle, for they were equipped with a single tiny pumper fire engine, a stretch of hose, a collection of gunny sacks and buckets, and their bare hands. The pumper was stationed three blocks to the south, alongside a narrow channel in from the Bay. It sucked up the water there and sent it along the hose to be played on the station walls and roof. Firemen ran their buckets back and forth between the Channel and the yard sheds. At the sheds, the sacks were dipped into the buckets and then smacked hard against the buildings' walls and roofs. At times, the firefighters must have thought that their efforts would eventually go to waste. The flames came so close to the station that the paint was blistered away from its walls and its window frames were set to smoldering. The shed roofs went afire time after time, new blazes breaking out as soon as old ones were stamped out.

But the stubborn firefighters refused to quit, with the result that the depot remained intact to play its part in the fine work done for the people of San Francisco by the Southern Pacific Railroad Company in the next nine days. Through it and the station over in Oakland millions of tons of medical supplies, food, blankets and clothing poured into the stricken city. And, through the two stations, more than 300,000 fleeing San Franciscans passed on their way to the safety promised in the homes of distant friends and relatives. All traveled free of charge.

3.

Most of those 300,000 people were jammed this Wednesday night into every one of San Francisco's western neighborhoods, stretching all the way from the western boundary of the Ham and Eggs fire to the Pacific beaches and north to the Golden Gate. Many were taken into homes that had remained intact through the quake. Most, however, with the memory of crashing walls and ceilings still fresh in their minds, preferred to remain outdoors. They were camped on sidewalks and in the streets. They were in small parks and squares and backyards. All about them were their belongings, ranging all the way from birdcages and suitcases to sewing machines and pianos. Here and there, fireplaces had been built of bricks from broken chimneys; smoke drifted up from them to mingle with the great clouds of smoke lumbering through the night sky from the burning downtown district; there was the aroma of coffee in the air. In places, some families had built tents of blankets and sheets. Children slept in them or in the arms of their mothers. One quake survivor later wrote that the western neighborhoods this night "had the look of the biggest camp ever built by man. You couldn't take a step without bumping into someone sitting on a curbstone or lying curled up asleep on the grass or the cobblestones. It seemed that more and more people kept crowding into the streets from other parts of the city every minute of the night."

There was an unending babble of voices throughout the night in that vast camp. Everyone had a story to tell. There was the family just arrived at Lafayette Square; they lived immediately west of Powell, and they said that they had buried their silverware in the backyard scant seconds before the fire took over their house; they planned to go back in the next days, dig up the silverware, rebuild their home and start life anew. There was the young boy near exhaustion; his home was in one of the western neighborhoods, and he had gone to help his crippled uncle, who resided close to the downtown district; he had put the old man into an armchair with casters on it and had wheeled him through the streets for several miles until he was able to place him in a makeshift hospital; after that, he had lost track of his uncle; he planned to search for him again in the morning. There was the man who had worked with a south-of-Market rescue party; he remembered hearing two trapped men comforting each other in a rubbled building; one had said, "Don't worry. Help is just outside. We'll get out all right"; moments later, fire had roared through the ruins. There was the woman who remembered seeing three hoodlums reach through the broken window of a liquor store and make off with as many bottles as they could carry while flames bore down on the place.

And, as is always the case in times of disaster, there were rumors—rumors of how badly the fire was going, rumors of looting, rumors of the numbers of people who had lost their lives, and rumors that the catastrophe had not limited itself to San Francisco alone, but had stretched its ugly hand all across the nation. There were those who said that thousands were dead and injured in the quake; there were those who said that at least three thousand people had perished in the Mechanics Pavilion fire alone—all of them the injured whom doctors and rescue workers had been unable to remove before the Ham and Eggs blaze swept through it. There were those who claimed that practically every American city had been left in ruins: The ground had given way under New Orleans and the Gulf of Mexico had surged through it; New York and Los Angeles had been shaken down; a tidal wave had smashed into Seattle; Chicago had fallen into Lake Michigan. Predictably and understandably, imaginations were running riot.

Just as imaginative were the rumors of thievery and looting in the city. One fantastic story held that a band of fourteen men attacked the Mint at the height of the fire around it, their aim being to break open the vaults and make off with as much as they could carry of the bullion and coin stored there. Soldiers, so the story went, shot them down as they charged up the stone steps to the front porch. The story, completely false, took such a grip on the city that it is still sometimes repeated as solid history.

And there were stories told in the red darkness of Wednesday night of the many thieves killed by soldiers. One often-repeated yarn concerned a well-dressed young man who was felled by a soldier when he was seen tugging at the fingers of a dead woman. He was found to have cut three of her ring-laden fingers away and put them in his pocket. Or so the story went.

Some people told of having seen the bodies of three hanged thieves dangling from lampposts on Market Street; others claimed that thieves could be found hanging from trees and posts in practically every park and square in town. Freely circulated was the tale of some burglars who were shot down when seen running from a building with their hats filled with coins. Just as freely circulated were the accounts of looters killed as they were caught reaching into broken store windows or sneaking from empty, ruined homes. One woman said that she had heard of a man who approached a group of soldiers to ask if he might take a final look at the body of his mother among some nearby corpses; the soldiers opened fire on him when they saw that, while bending over the woman in apparent grief, he was actually trying to chew the earrings from her ears; in the next days, the story was reported as fact in several newspapers across the nation, among them the *Chicago American*. Many people complained of having their pockets picked or their purses snatched away during the day.

Most, if not all, of the rumors circulated that night were shown to be false in the weeks and months following the

quake. All that is really known today is that Schmitz early
Wednesday morning mentioned the killing of three looters
to his police commissioners and that General Funston later
said that two looters had been reported to him as shot; no
one knows whether they were talking about the same men.
It is assumed that there must have been, in the excitement
of the day, several street executions. But the exact number
of thieves who met their death that Wednesday remains
undetermined. Some newspapers of the time—and very few
immediate news accounts of the quake and its aftermath
can be trusted, as will soon be seen—set the figure as high
as a couple of hundred, while others put it as low as ten or
twenty. One other fact, though, can be safely assumed:
pickpockets had a field day for a time in the surging mobs
hurrying away from the fires.

But, on that Wednesday, most people were not yet
thinking clearly, and they accepted the rumors without
question and were terrified by them. One survivor, then a
little child, recalls today that her mother concealed a valuable music box under a small pile of bricks and then sat by
it through the night. A man and wife expressed their fear
of returning to their flat in the downtown district; somehow, they kept forgetting that it was probably burned to
the ground and were concerned only that some thief had
probably made off with their best dishware, a family heir-
loom. One young boy later recalled that, as he was driving
a wagon through the streets early in the day, he stopped to
give a middle-aged woman a ride. She was expensively
dressed and had obviously been injured in the quake, for
her left hand was swathed in bandage. After a while, apparently coming to trust the youngster, she suddenly told
him that she was not really hurt, but was wearing the

bandage as a camouflage. She undid it just enough for him to see that it contained a fortune in jewels.

It must not be thought, however, that terror was an all-consuming emotion in the street camps that night. It was not. Mingled with it were defiance and even gaiety. Granted, the people were shaken and exhausted, and thus vulnerable to all the frightening rumors, but they were in the main a hardy breed, filled with all the toughness and high spirit of the early westerner. With but a few exceptions, that toughness and spirit had seen them through the tragic day without panic. Now, in the red-splashed night, those two strengths were quick to show themselves.

And so it was that many a curbside listener thrust the rumors aside and spoke optimistically of the future. Some predicted that, in the morning, they would get safely away to distant friends and relatives. Others shook their heads defiantly; escape was not for them. They would stay right here and see this thing through, come what may. Then they would get down to the job of rebuilding their homes or businesses and starting life anew.

Here and there, laughter erupted as people, with the very human trait of finding comedy in the midst of tragedy, recalled some silly sight or incident of the day—perhaps the remembered glimpse of a stunned quake victim in nightshirt and top hat, perhaps the recollection of witlessly grabbing up some useless household knick-knack and leaving behind food and clothing as homes were abandoned. Two men who had helped fight the fire in the financial district chuckled as they recalled an incident at one building about to be dynamited. As soldiers were getting ready to set their charges, a well-known religious fanatic had suddenly appeared in an upper story window.

His long white beard contrasting sharply with the yellow air, he had screamed that the wrath of God would descend upon any and all who laid hands on the building, killing them instantly. The startled soldiers fled in all directions.

There was much politeness everywhere. As is characteristic of people sharing a tragedy, the refugees were careful of each other's feelings. Most of those who had food shared it with less fortunate strangers. Sleepers did not cry out in anger when new arrivals stumbled over them. Many a tired mother and father patiently played guessing games with their children or told them stories when the youngsters were too upset or too excited to sleep. At one intersection, a man parked a treasure that he had managed to remove from his home. It was an upright piano, and two young ladies climbed up on it and entertained the surrounding crowd with songs. In a small park, several couples danced to the accompaniment of an accordion.

It is well that toughness, defiance and gaiety were on the scene that night. They helped to keep many a San Franciscan from dwelling too long on the great sense of helplessness that he must have felt at the core of his being. He was homeless and he knew that days and weeks and, perhaps, months would pass before real order returned to his life. He had little or no idea of how he was going to feed himself and his family tomorrow morning and, most likely, for many mornings to come, for he realized that he depended much on the outside world for help—and he still had no way of knowing how much of that world was still standing and how much was down in a heap like his own. He could not say if disease and starvation would stalk the city in the next days. At this moment, life seemed to hold but one certainty. The disaster had not yet run its full course by a long shot. The red sky told him that every time he looked at it.

## 4.

Thousands of San Franciscans might not have felt so helpless had they known that, since early that Wednesday, the news of the disaster had been spreading over the whole nation like wildfire, reaching out then across the seas, and that a giant wave of assistance was beginning to take shape. It was to come flooding into San Francisco from every direction—from the United States and California governments, from large cities and small towns in every state, and from more than a dozen foreign nations.

At the U.S. government level, the news of the quake reached Secretary of War William Howard Taft before midday. He rushed over to the White House and, with President Theodore Roosevelt, drew up a request to Congress for $500,000 in relief for the stricken city. It was passed by the House of Representatives that afternoon and by the Senate the next morning. Congress also granted the Army permission to use any and all of its supplies in aiding San Francisco.

Then, when Funston's two telegrams arrived that night, Taft ordered 200,000 rations—each equal to one day's worth of food for one person—sent south from Vancouver Barracks. Taft then instructed the Army's Quartermaster Corps to telegraph every military post in the country and have them dispatch all available tents to San Francisco without delay. Finally, he telegraphed Funston to "do everything possible to assist in keeping order in saving life and property and in relieving hunger by use of troops, material and supplies under your order."

The red-bearded little General had been doing this very thing through the day and night. But now, at least, he had the sanction of the Secretary of War for his actions.

The Army was not the only branch of the service to swing into action. Sailors and marines from surrounding bases had immediately rushed into the city to join with soldiers in keeping order. By Thursday morning, they would be augmented by the men of the Navy's Pacific Squadron. News of the disaster reached the squadron's ships early Wednesday as they were sailing off San Diego near California's southern border. They immediately headed for San Francisco, moving at full speed through the day and night.

At the state level, Governor Pardee hurried the hundred miles from his Sacramento office to Oakland, where he set up temporary headquarters to organize relief work for San Francisco. He called out the state militia and sent them into the city to provide whatever assistance was necessary.

In cities and towns throughout this country and abroad, steps immediately got under way to send aid westward. The result was a tidal wave of money and goods that, in a matter of days, amounted to several million dollars in value.

Every item in the great flood of assistance that was taking shape by Wednesday night would be needed—and needed desperately. By midnight, most of the downtown district lay in ruins and close to 175,000 people were homeless. But there was more havoc to come.

# Chapter Eight

# THURSDAY MORNING

## 1.

JUST AS THE EXHAUSTED FIREMEN had feared, the crown of Nob Hill, with all its great mansions, was marked for doom within minutes after the roaring flames jumped Powell at Bush Street at three o'clock Thursday morning. The flames swirled wildly westward to Mason Street, a single block over from Powell, and then, even as they continued farther west, they sent one arm racing north to the top up the hill. By four o'clock the fire was coming through the backyards of the great homes there.

Among the largest of those homes was one built in the latter years of the nineteenth century by Mark Hopkins, the Sacramento hardware store operator who became a millionaire by joining with Charles Crocker, Leland Stanford and Collis Huntington to build the Central Pacific Railroad. The home stood on the south side of California Street between Powell and Mason and was visible from all parts of the downtown district. Several years before the quake, on the death of his wife, Hopkins gave the building to the University of California, and it became the Hopkins Art Institute. In 1906, it contained thousands of dollars worth of paintings and statues.

The art treasures were the cause of much activity

throughout Wednesday and the first hours of Thursday.
Institute teachers and students—joined by a student delega-
tion from the university's Berkeley campus across the
Bay—shoved their way through the crowds on Nob Hill
and removed several hundred pictures and statues to the
front lawn, afterward hauling away as many as possible to
other parts of town, carrying them on their shoulders,
pushing them along in barrows. Navy men arrived to lend
a hand sometime in the night.

Though many of the art treasures made their way to
safety, a large number had to be abandoned on the front
lawn and within the building when the fire finally crashed
into its west wing sometime after dawn Thursday. Others
were moved across California Street to the grounds of the
James Flood mansion. They were destroyed right along
with that great home.

In charge of the Navy men lending a hand was a young
lieutenant named McMillan. Shortly before dawn, he saw
that there were not enough Institute people and sailors to
get the last of the art treasures away from the lawn and out
of the house before the roaring flames were all over the
place. He began to enlist extra workers from among the
men in the crowds still thronging California Street. He did
so with the assistance of an ugly-looking service pistol.

John Castillo Kennedy's *The Great Earthquake and
Fire* tells how he handled any men who balked at the idea
of going near or into a building about to explode in flame:

> . . . "Here, you fellows," he barked at a group of on-
> lookers. "Hurry in there and get those paintings out."
> There was no reply. The lieutenant's long pistol came
> up. "Now you get over there, all of you, and hustle those
> paintings out. And I mean business."

"Are—are you swearing in deputies?" one man asked nervously.

"I don't have to swear 'em in when I need them," McMillan snapped. "I swear at them. Now git!"

Ordering one man after another into the building, he came to a fat man who protested, "But I'm a member of the Humane Society. See, here's my badge."

"This is humane work," McMillan told him shortly. "Get on in there and get busy."

A few moments later, McMillan ran into a heavy-set man who did not like the idea of being commanded to do anything. Kennedy reports the encounter this way:

. . . "What business have you got to order us around?"

"You see this gun?" Lieutenant McMillan asked him. "Well, I think it's aimed right at your eye. Now come here, I want to have a little talk with you."

No talk was necessary; the gun carried its own message. "All right, boss," the man said quickly, and hurried into the house.

While the men scuttled back and forth with their arms loaded with paintings and statuary, firefighters, using a cistern on the property, played streams of water over the massive wooden house. A fire captain later recalled that, during the predawn hours, "we were visited by His Honor the Mayor, who came up into the building to encourage us in our good work, and left orders to work our best in trying to save the Institute."

But all the good work was to no avail. The Hopkins mansion was soon ablaze, followed by the neighboring home of Leland Stanford, the founder of Stanford University. Then the Huntington and Crocker places went. The latter sported a seventy-six-foot-high tower. It blazed like a beacon in the smoky morning sky. San Francisco's greatest homes were dissolving to ash.

There was one building on the hilltop that firemen thought might withstand the fire. It was the giant Fairmont Hotel, nearing completion on the northwest corner of Powell and Mason. It was being built at a cost of $5,000,000, and—sprawling thing of granite and marble and concrete that it was—the firefighters thought it could fend off any onslaught, just as the Mint and Post Office had done. They did not know, however, about all the gallons of paint that were stored in the place for finishing off its several hundred rooms. Blistering waves of heat reached the paint. It went off with the roar of an exploding bomb, and the hotel turned itself into a torch.

The Flood mansion, surrounded by a fence of bronze, stood on the same side of California as the Fairmont. Flames spread quickly to it from the hotel. A Hopkins Institute professor dashed among the paintings and statuary piled about the Flood yard. There was no chance of getting them all to safety now. He knelt before several pictures, knifed their canvases free of the frames and rolled them under his arm. Then, with the great house a roaring inferno above his head, he ran for his life.

The whole hilltop was afire now. Nothing remained to hold the holocaust back from the northern section of the city.

Thursday was a sunny spring day, but there was no way of knowing it in central San Francisco. Smoke towered above the city to an estimated height of two miles, blotting out all view of the sky. Through the black rolling clouds, the flashes of red that were the burning Nob Hill homes were visible for blocks in all directions and were watched by thousands of people. Among them was writer Jack London.

San Francisco-born London was at his home in Sonoma County north of San Francisco when the earthquake struck. He and his wife immediately set out for the city. A letter written some days later to a friend gives a capsule review of his experiences that fateful day.

Dear Merle,

You bet I was in the thick of it. Routed out of bed at quarter past five, half an hour later Mrs. London and I were in the saddle. We rode miles over the surrounding country. An hour after the shock, from a high place in the mountains, we could see at the same time the smoke of burning San Francisco and burning Santa Rosa . . . on Wednesday afternoon we got into San Francisco and spent the whole night in the path of the flames—you bet I saw it all! I'm glad all of you escaped O.K. Do I understand you are going to move to Oakland?

Affectionately,
Your Uncle Jack

Then, in the pages of the magazine *Current Literature*, London wrote these impressions of the first fiery night in San Francisco:

. . . Wednesday night, while the whole city crashed and roared into ruin, was a quiet night. There were no crowds. There was no shouting and yelling. There was no hysteria, no disorder. I passed Wednesday in the path of the advancing flames, and in all those terrible hours, I saw not one woman who wept, not one man who was excited, not one person who was in the slightest degree panic-stricken. . . .

At first glance, London's observation that there were no crowds in the streets seems strange and inconsistent with the fact that there were about 200,000 homeless people loose in the city. He was obviously talking of the downtown streets already on fire or facing immediate destruction. He would have had to change his mind by nine o'clock Thursday morning, for by then the downtown streets not actually ablaze were choked with traffic, moving east and west at the same time.

The people hurrying west were from the neighborhoods between Powell and Van Ness. Most of them had remained at their homes and apartments and hotels and stores through the night. Now, with the great wall of flame that had jumped Powell sweeping toward them, they were being hustled westward on the rough commands of soldiers. The soldiers did not endear themselves to the hearts of many people in these neighborhoods that morning. They were so impatient to clear the streets that they gave some householders no time to collect belongings or food before pushing them on. A number of residents argued that their homes were still some blocks distant; the flames would be several hours reaching them and might even be stopped before then. They wanted to stay where they were. They might even be able to do something to protect their property. The soldiers pushed them on, sometimes at bayonet point.

There were, however, certain people in the area that no one could move until they themselves were ready to be on their way. These were the men, women and children who flocked around groceries and delicatessens to get their hands on any food available. The stores reacted differently to the crowds. Some sold their goods at outrageous prices. The doors of others were thrown open—their owners knowing that they were doomed—and the people were allowed to storm through them to take whatever they wished. Some merchants organized and marshaled their employees and handed out their goods in orderly fashion, sometimes charging for them, sometimes not. One store-keeper devised an unusual method of distribution; he nailed boards across his shop window, leaving a slight gap along the center line; people were welcome to anything that they could reach through the gap. Not a few shop-keepers made the mistake of locking their places and pull-ing the blinds or boarding over the windows. The people simply broke in and ransacked the shelves. One merchant planted himself in front of his door and ordered the crowds away. A soldier pulled him aside and motioned the people inside.

Most of the eastward-moving crowds were making their way to Market Street and thence to either the Ferry Build-ing or the Southern Pacific Station; from the former they would sail to the safety of East Bay towns, with some then traveling on to other parts of the state or the country; at the latter they would board the Los Angeles-bound trains that had started to run at dawn. As they entered Market, they saw smoking ruins on both sides of the street, with the glare of a few remaining fires showing here and there. Cu-rious eyes glanced down Sixth Street and glimpsed dishev-eled soldiers sitting on the Mint steps, rifles across their knees. Many people left Market and surged up to the Post Office with letters for distant relatives and friends, at first certain that there was no hope of getting them sent and then surprised to find clerks on duty and wagons being loaded with mail sacks. Smoke still poured thickly from the *Call* Building dome, although, as seen through its gap-ing windows, there seemed to be nothing left of the build-ing's insides. Across the way, fire was still at work on the *Chronicle* Building. The marquee of the Columbia Thea-

ter was a mass of twisted black metal. All along the great
street, lampposts had turned soft with the heat and were
now arched over so that many of their tops were touching
the sidewalk. Great masses of smoke moved sluggishly
across the sky, looking as if some hideous storm was about
to break right above the rooftop. The air was thick and
gray, and many people had handkerchiefs tied across their
noses.

Those who reached the Ferry Building found that it and
the docks stretching away to either side looked odd and out
of place amidst all the destruction, unburned as they were.
The gutters of East Street, which ran along their front,
were overflowing with all the Bay water that had been
poured on them through yesterday and last night. The
stone steps leading up to the Ferry Building were jammed
with people and their possessions, as were its inner corridors. Here and there, bundles of clothing and odd bits of
household ware lay deserted by their owners. Policemen
stood in cordons throughout the building, shaping the
people into lines and moving them steadily toward the
slips out back. Ferry whistles hooted interminably as the
little boats made one trip after the other across the Bay to
Oakland. The people in line made little noise. They
shuffled forward, each patiently waiting his turn to go
aboard.

There was one emotional outburst during the morning.
Enrico Caruso, his autographed photo of Teddy Roosevelt
still tucked under his arm and his dark topcoat littered
with ash, hurried into the building and started through
one of the police lines. Immediately, a blue-sleeved arm
swept across his chest, stopping him in midstep. And just
where did he think he was going? The singer shouted his
name and, purpling with rage, demanded to be let through

to get a launch that the Metropolitan Opera Company had chartered for the trip across the Bay. Most of the singers were already aboard. He had to get through. They just might not wait for him all day. The policeman, joined by a couple of fellow officers, shook his head in anger and disbelief. This was the great Enrico Caruso? He didn't look like an opera singer. Some people would use any name just to reach the head of the line before everyone else.

Enraged, Caruso spent a moment trying to prove his identity. Then out from under his arm came the Roosevelt photograph. He waved it under the hard police faces and shouted, "See? See?" Who else but a famous man would have such a picture? Skepticism faded, and the policemen waved him through. He bustled out to the slip, his valet hurrying along behind him with a couple of valises. The singer located the launch and climbed aboard. The boat roared toward Oakland and the start of Caruso's trip back to New York.

There is a San Francisco legend that, as the launch sped away, he turned to shake his fist at the burning city.

## 2.

The very same ferries that were hauling people away from the city at the rate of seventy a minute were also, on their return trips, bringing an increasing number of men into San Francisco. These were newspaper reporters converging in increasing number on the city, via Oakland and other East Bay ports, from all over the country. The first of their number had arrived yesterday, and General Funston had assigned them an office at the docks as their headquarters. Beyond that, he had given them no cooperation. He had issued orders that no one, unless on official business, was to enter the city, and he had made sure that they were extended to cover the press. It was well known that, for some reason in his past, he harbored no love for newsmen and didn't want them underfoot. However, using Oakland facilities, they had wired word of Funston's stand to their editors, who, in turn, complained to the War Department. The department got a message to Funston, requesting him to issue passes into the city for the reporters. Funston, perhaps thinking some acid thoughts along the way, did so. He even established a press headquarters at Fort Mason.

Free to move within the city, the reporters let loose with an unending stream of stories on the quake and its aftermath. Theirs was the first genuine word to the outside world of the situation in the city. Until they got to work, newspapers across the country and abroad had to depend on rumors and fragmented telegraph reports from East Bay towns for their accounts of the quake and fire. Some printed false stories of riots. Some said the fire was under control. And some used their imagination, guessing at the number of people who were killed and injured and giving fanciful descriptions of the fire. William Bronson, in *The Earth Shook, The Sky Burned*, writes that "one Chicago editor heard that the city was on fire and ordered his writers to, '. . . burn the whole town down!' " Many papers, however, simply and truthfully told their readers that there was no news as yet from the stricken city.

Outside reporters were, of course, not the only newsmen active in the city that day. Working side by side with them were members of San Francisco's shattered newspaper industry, all of them doing their jobs while fear for their families and homes lurked at the back of their mind. In fact, they had been at work since the day before, and one of the city's five papers—the afternoon *Daily News*, whose offices were just outside the downtown district—had managed to put out a Wednesday edition late in the day.

Its largest headline read "HUNDREDS DEAD!" Its secondary head, covering three lines, thundered "FIRE FOLLOWS EARTHQUAKE, LAYING DOWNTOWN SECTION IN RUINS—CITY SEEMS DOOMED FOR LACK OF WATER." Much of the front page was devoted to a list of known dead and injured, beginning with these fatalities on record at Mechanics Pavilion:

> Max Fenner, policeman, killed in collapse Essex Hotel.
> Niece of Detective Dillon, killed in collapse, 6th and Shipley.
> Unidentified woman, killed at 18 7th St.
> Two unknown men, brought in autos.

Of the events of the day, the *News* reported:

> . . . Thousands of men who went to bed wealthy last night awoke this morning practically bankrupt.
> . . . The people are appalled, terror-stricken. Thousands, fearful of a recurrence of the dreadful disaster, with results still more dire, are hastening out of San Francisco.
> . . . The fury of the tremblor was greater than any that has been known in the history of the city.
> . . . At least forty buildings were aflame within ten minutes after the tremblor passed.
> . . . A building collapsed at Steiner and Haight Sts. No report of loss of life.
> . . . Along Market St. . . . the sidewalks are literally strewn with wreckage. In many places the sidewalks have collapsed, falling into basements.
> . . . The Majestic Theater is almost a complete wreck.

The *Daily News* was a young paper, just four years old at the time, and its Wednesday edition was a fine achievement. But a far more unusual newspaper hit the streets on Thursday. In fact, it probably ranks as the most unusual paper ever issued in San Francisco's history. Four pages long, it was a combined edition of the city's three burned-out morning dailies—the *Call*, *Chronicle* and *Examiner*. Making it truly unique was the fact that it was published by reporters and editors who had spent their lives in deadly competition with each other and that the job was done without the permission of the owners of the three papers. The reporters and editors didn't bother to ask for such permission, knowing full well that they probably wouldn't be able to locate their bosses anyway.

The little paper began to take shape when *Call*, *Chronicle* and *Examiner* reporters and editors began to assemble at the as-yet-unburned offices of the afternoon *Bulletin*, a few blocks north on Kearny Street from Market. The *Examiner* and *Call* men said that their buildings were already afire. The *Bulletin* and *Chronicle* men answered that they were in trouble, too. There was no power to run their presses, and the fires from the financial district would soon be threatening their buildings. These rival newspapermen stared at each other in anger and frustration. Here they were, sitting in the middle of the century's biggest story, right in their own city, and there was no way for them to get a word into print about it.

They were not given too much time to dwell on their misfortune. The financial district fires soon were pressing in on the *Bulletin* Building, and the men inside had to move off. Out in the street, several reporters and editors from the trio of morning papers got together and decided to stop feeling angry and get down to work. They agreed to cross the Bay and see if they could put out a combined issue on the presses of the *Oakland Tribune*. Hours later, when, dirty and disheveled, they descended on the *Tribune*, the presses there were put at their disposal. And so, without even stopping to think about seeking the permission of the *Call*, *Chronicle* and *Examiner* owners, they worked through the night on their paper, filling it with stories from bedraggled reporters who, hearing what was being done, came hurrying over to the *Tribune* from all parts of San Francisco.

On Thursday, the finished product was shipped across to San Francisco. It was sold along streets and in parks and squares and on doorsteps for ten cents or was handed out free to anyone without money. People grabbed at every copy in sight and hungrily devoured the words. Here, under a two-line headline announcing EARTHQUAKE AND FIRE: SAN FRANCISCO IN RUINS, is what they read in the lead story:

> Death and destruction have been the fate of San Francisco. Shaken by a tremblor at 5:13 o'clock yesterday morning, the shock lasting 48 seconds, and scourged by flames that raged diametrically in all directions, the city is a mass of smouldering ruins. At six o'clock last evening the flames seemingly playing with increased vigor, threatened to destroy such sections as their fury had spared during the earlier portion of the day. . . .
>
> After darkness, thousands of the homeless were making their way with their blankets and scant provisions to Golden Gate Park and the beach to find shelter. Those in the homes on the hills just north of the Hayes Valley wrecked section piled their belongings in the streets and express wagons and automobiles were hauling the things away to the sparsely settled regions. Everybody in San

Francisco is prepared to leave the city, for the belief is firm that San Francisco will be totally destroyed.

. . . It is estimated that the loss in San Francisco will reach from $150,000,000 to $200,000,000. These figures are in the rough and nothing can be told until partial accounting is taken.

On every side, there was death and suffering yesterday. Hundreds were injured either burned, crushed or struck by falling pieces from the buildings and one of ten died while on the operating table at Mechanics Pavilion, improvised as a hospital for the comfort and care of 300 of the injured. The number of dead is not known but it is estimated that at least 500 met their death in the horror.

At nine o'clock, under a special message from President Roosevelt, the city was placed under martial law. Hundreds of troops patrolled the streets and drove the crowds back, while hundreds more were set to work assisting the fire and police departments. . . .

The water supply was entirely cut off, and may be it was just as well for the lines of the fire department would have been absolutely useless at any stage . . . early in the morning it was seen that the only possible chance to save the city lay in effort to check the flames by the use of dynamite. During the day a blast could be heard in any section at intervals of only a few minutes, and buildings not destroyed by fire were blown to atoms. But through the gaps made the flames jumped. . . . Men worked like fiends to combat the laughing, roaring, onrushing fire demon.

Other stories in the paper bore such dramatic headlines as "NO HOPE LEFT FOR SAFETY OF ANY BUILDINGS," "WHOLE CITY IS ABLAZE," "CHURCH OF ST. IGNATIUS IS DESTROYED" and "BLOW BUILDINGS UP TO CHECK FLAMES."

The little paper, hurriedly prepared by men who must have been emotionally and physically exhausted by the time it went to press, is not a prime example of complete accuracy. For instance, firemen undoubtedly would have had something to say about the statement that "may be it was just as well" there was no water. President Roosevelt would have been surprised to know that he put the city under martial law at nine o'clock—and, incidentally, the paper doesn't specify whether it was nine in the morning or nine at night; the reference, however, seems to be to the morning because of the sentences that follow on the use of soldiers to control the crowds and assist the firemen. If so, then Roosevelt knew little or nothing of the quake's havoc by that time. And, at any rate, he never put the city under martial law at any point.

But these flaws are understandable, considering the circumstances under which it was prepared. What really counts is that it remains to this day a testament to the energy and determination of a handful of men.

3.

By noontime Thursday, Mayor Eugene Schmitz had not slept or rested for thirty-one hours. Outwardly, he was little more than the ghost of the man San Francisco knew so well. His customarily immaculate clothing was rumpled and stained; his tie was loose, his collar wrinkled; his shoes were caked with mud and cracked from walking through too much water. His face was dead white, his eyes bloodshot, his hair tangled. His hands were trembling.

But, inwardly, he was twice the man he had been. All traces of the jovial backslapping politician were gone, burned away completely, as if they were paper buildings

that had got in the way of the downtown fires. All that
was left in him now was that terrible sense of responsibility
to his city and its people. It consumed him. It kept him on
his feet with nothing more to sustain him than an occa-
sional cup of coffee. It drove him to fury with anyone who
moaned that the whole city was doomed—and, this morning, more and more of the men about him were saying just
that.

That fury glittered hard in his red-rimmed eyes now as
he listened to his fire commissioners give their latest reports on the fires. Things, they said, were as bad as they
had been yesterday. Even worse. At least 200,000 people
were homeless. The count of known dead was over three
hundred, and only God knew how many others had perished in fallen and burned buildings. Two thirds of central San Francisco had gone up in smoke. More was going
by the minute.

Below Market, the South of the Slot fire and the southern arm of the Ham and Eggs fire were now into the
crowded Mission District, that sprawling neighborhood of
laborers and middle-class workers. People were fleeing in
all directions from the path of the flames. Firemen and
their little engines had chased the flames all through the
night, trying to stop or slow them at a dozen points with
cistern water, sewage and dynamite. They had failed at
every turn of the way, falling back always, blistered and
blackened, before the raging heat. The flames were now
burning deep into the district along a five-block-wide
front, between Howard Street on the east and Dolores
Street on the west. If the whole district fell, San Francisco
would have another 50,000 homeless people on its hands.

So far as the rest of the fires below Market were concerned, the news was a little better. Over on the east, their

southward march had been held away from the harbor by a distance of one to three blocks along an irregular line down to Townsend Street. There, they had been kept from getting into the Southern Pacific Station. And although they had gutted Townsend all the way east from Second to Eighth, they had not been able to sweep farther south. But there was no telling what the next hours might bring.

"What about north of Market?" he asked grimly.

The answers came flatly and tonelessly.

First, the run of the fire from the financial district was, as Schmitz knew, well past Powell. It was moving westward along a front that stretched from Geary Street on the south clear up to the top of Nob Hill on the north. The front was an irregular one as it cut its way toward Van Ness Avenue. At some points, it was only three blocks away from Van Ness; in others, it was still four and five blocks distant. But is was moving steadily. The guess was that it would come up to Van Ness by late this afternoon or early tonight.

Next, the arm of the fire that had spread over Nob Hill at dawn was now fanning out in three directions:

"West toward Van Ness," said one commissioner. "North toward Russian Hill. And back northeast toward Telegraph Hill."

Schmitz clenched his fists. When was this whole thing going to stop? No nightmare could last forever. Perhaps those who said the whole city was doomed were right. He caught himself and shook his head. No, that couldn't be!

"And the Delmonico fire?" he made himself ask.

The Mayor already knew the answer to that one, the commissioners said. Its northern arm had joined with the financial district fire to sweep through Chinatown and over Nob Hill. Its southern arm, after jumping Powell, had roared west to join the north-of-Market section of the Ham and Eggs fire. The whole area south from Geary to Market and west from Powell to Van Ness was gutted. The City Hall was still blazing; some 85,000 city records were going up in smoke; they would smolder for days.

Out beyond Van Ness, the Ham and Eggs fire had been held from burning west of Octavia Street, just a block over from its birthplace. This was another tiny bit of good news in the midst of complete chaos.

Schmitz was seated at a table in the latest of his headquarters, a small dancing and meeting place called Franklin Hall. Located on Fillmore Street, seven blocks west of Van Ness, it was his fourth "office" since leaving the Hall of Justice. He had settled in at the Fairmont Hotel, but was driven from there shortly before dawn, after which he had stationed himself for a time at an intersection somewhere along Van Ness. Then he had tried the North End Police Station on Washington Street, just a half-block off Van Ness, moving on to his present quarters when he found the place too small for all the people working with him.

Franklin Hall was now jammed to capacity with those workers. Secretaries and members of his city staff were at tables all over the place. Messengers lounged against walls or napped in corners. Someone was making coffee. The air was heavy with cigar and pipe smoke—and with the heat and smoke that crept in under every door and through every crack in the building. Crowded around Schmitz, along with the fire commissioners, were some fire and police officers, a sprinkling of Army and Navy men, and members of the Committee of Safety. There were just a few of the latter, for most of the committeemen were now away from Franklin Hall, having been sent out on a variety of relief jobs just a while ago. Schmitz smiled to himself, recalling that quite a few men who had not showed up for yesterday's first committee meeting had put in an appearance this morning. It was good to think that more and more of San Francisco's leading citizens were putting aside their personal animosity for him and springing to their city's aid. He gauged that the committee must now number fifty of the eighty men originally invited to join it.

But he had no illusions about these men. He knew that their old scorn and hatred would return as soon as the days of crisis were over and that many of them would resume their campaign to get him kicked out of office and brought to trial for graft. For the moment, though, they obeyed his every order without flinching, and that was all that counted.

And he had come up with many an order for them today, without wasting any time in being polite in giving his instructions:

Go out, find all the volunteer help you can lay hands on and gather every available scrap of food in the city. Begin arranging for its distribution to the homeless.

Send some wagons to find meat and flour in the towns just to the south. See what food can be found in East Bay towns.

Find all the bakeries still standing in the city and get them back into operation.

Assist the soldiers in carrying out this morning's order by General Funston to collect all corpses still in the streets and bury them before they cause the start and spread of disease.

Investigate the growing talk that rats, fleeing ahead of the fires, are invading the street and park "camps."

Find disinfectant for use by the homeless in the next days.

Hunt up tents and cots for the refugees.

Schmitz sat back for a moment and looked at the men surrounding him, especially those of his committeemen. The news that he now had for them would undoubtedly tax their patience to the breaking point.

He began to speak, slowly. Van Ness Avenue, he pointed out, was the broadest street in the city, one hundred and twenty-five feet wide. It was here that the next main line of defense must be drawn—from Golden Gate Avenue at the edge of the Ham and Eggs fire on the south to Fort Mason at the Bay's edge on the north. The line of defense would stretch twenty-five blocks.

He took a deep breath. The hard part was coming now. To strengthen the line of defense, he said, he was going to order that every building on the east side of Van Ness all along that twenty-five-block stretch be dynamited. Then, before the arrival of the flames from the downtown district and Nob Hill, the firemen were somehow to put out every blaze caused by the dynamiting and were to level as much of the debris as possible. The width of the street and the rubbled buildings would create a gap too broad for the wildest of fires to jump. Also, because the dynamiting would extend right up to the Bay, the approaching fires would not be able to work their way north around the gap.

As he had expected, there was a storm of protest. The plan, they said flatly, was foolhardy; it called for the destruction of several million dollars' worth of the city's finest homes; many of them—and this is what made his words so difficult and the protest so predictable—were occupied by the Committee of Safety members and their families. Why not, the men argued, continue with yesterday's policy of dynamiting only those buildings adjacent to the fires? Why not expend every effort to halt the flames *before* they reached Van Ness?

Schmitz let the storm run its course. Then, his voice hard, he told the men that, if they stopped long enough to think about it, they already knew the answers to their questions. First, yesterday's dynamiting of adjacent buildings had been a waste of time, succeeding only in giving the fires more fuel on which to feed. Second, everybody in this room knew full well that there was not a hope in the world of stopping the fires before they reached Van Ness. If they had forgotten this fact, they were invited to walk over to Van Ness right now and take a good look at the eastern skyline.

His voice softened. He reminded the men that yesterday he and the police commissioners had been the ones to order that young Army officer, Lieutenant Briggs, to dynamite only those structures alongside the fires. He said that he had known full well that distant dynamiting would have made more effective firebreaks, but that he had feared the wrath of the city had the flames burned themselves out before reaching the distant firebreaks. Well, that had been a mistake and he wasn't going to repeat it. He was now going to make the best firebreak possible, regardless of the cost to Van Ness.

If he didn't, the whole western area of the city was doomed—beginning with the Western Addition, the vast middle-class neighborhood that abutted the full length of Van Ness and stretched all the way out to Golden Gate Park. It was home for 150,000 people, and once the flames were through it, they would spear into the Richmond District to the west and the Sunset District to the southwest.

After they had done their work there—well, there would be no more San Francisco.

Schmitz stood up. Did the men here at this table want to gamble with the fate of the rest of the city by trying to spare a stretch of homes that were doomed anyway?

He got no answer.

Did anyone here have a better idea as to how to stop the fires?

Again no answer.

Schmitz said, "Then it's settled, gentlemen."

He turned to Assistant Fire Chief Dougherty and an Army officer. He gave his first instructions for the destruction of Van Ness Avenue.

# Chapter Nine

# THE LAST STANDS

## 1.

THE INSTRUCTIONS WERE SIMPLE.

To Assistant Chief Dougherty: Order all firemen—except those in the Mission District—to assemble their equipment along Van Ness. Have them get what rest they can as soon as they're in place. They'll have their hands full once the dynamiting starts. Short of a miracle, there will be no sleep again for anyone tonight.

To the Army officer: Send some of your soldiers into the streets between the fires and Van Ness. Have them move out the remaining people as fast as possible; tell them not to waste time listening to any arguments about families being afraid to move away or wanting to stay and protect their property; they're to get everyone out, even if they have to carry them. Then they're to clear the houses along the east side of Van Ness, the doomed houses. Send the rest of your men just west of Van Ness. Have them tell the residents to open their windows so the glass won't shatter with the concussion of the blasting.

Still more to the officer: There probably isn't enough dynamite left in this city to add up to a good-sized firecracker. Commandeer a boat, a fast one if possible. Send it across the Bay to pick up any dynamite it can find. Have

*143*

it return to Fort Mason at the northern end of Van Ness.
Have wagons ready there to bring the stuff down Van
Ness.

The two men nodded and, without a question, hurried
from the building. Schmitz followed them out a few minutes later, after assigning further relief duties to the Committee of Safety members. He paused to stare angrily at the
filthy yellow-black clouds rolling at least two miles skyward, and he thought that he could feel the heat of the
fires clear over here on Fillmore Street. He got into his
carriage and rode to Van Ness to watch the arrival of the
firemen.

Within thirty minutes, they began to appear, staggering
out of cross streets to park their grimed and overworked
engines along the west side of the wide boulevard. Some
stretched their hoses out to nearby hydrants, hoping
against hope that the city's water mains, which had been
under repair all night, would soon have water again.
Others went in search of underground cisterns, while still
others began knocking at doors to see if any householders
had wells or private cisterns to which hoses could be
linked.

Then, in the very moment that their preparations were
done, they sank down to rest. They picked their spots at
random. Most lay down by their engines, pulled their caps
or helmets over their faces and went immediately to sleep.
Others sprawled in the gutters, joined by those who sat on
the curbs and, with their hands dangling from their knees,
let their chins fall to their chests. There were some,
though, who were too keyed up to rest. They lounged
against the engines and talked of their disgust with their
impotence in the face of roaring flames and of the hope-
lessness of stopping them at Van Ness. Now and again,

these men reached out to pat the firehorses that stood close to complete exhaustion in their traces.

Schmitz walked slowly among the sleeping firemen nearest at hand. Their boots were caked with mud and ash, and their uniforms were filthy, often torn, now and again streaked with the dry blood of some injury suffered sometime in the last thirty or thirty-one hours. Their faces were black with grime and were blistered, as were their hands. Schmitz saw that they slept as if they were dead, some flat on their backs, with their mouths wide open and their eyes sunk deep into their heads. Now and again, one man or another would shudder convulsively. The Mayor wondered how anyone would ever wake them when the time came and how they would ever be able to get to their feet.

Soon after the arrival of the firemen, the people being cleared from the streets to the east began entering Van Ness in increasing numbers. From a distance, they looked no different from all the homeless of yesterday morning. They carried their belongings on their back or in cloth bags or suitcases, or they pushed them along in anything from baby carriages to wheelchairs and toy wagons. Some walked slowly and dazedly and others hurried along, just like the crowds of yesterday.

But when the first of the people drew near, Schmitz sighted something that had not been present yesterday. There was anger in many of them, some of it blind and illogical, some of it legitimate—blind and illogical in those who, without any real firefighting equipment at their disposal, wanted to defend their little homes against a towering inferno; legitimate in those who complained that they had been driven out of their neighborhoods without being given the chance to grab up the last foodstocks in stores there. Schmitz swore under his breath. The soldiers need not have been in *that much* of a hurry. The food problem was critical and would probably get worse before it got better.

Most of the people surged past him and moved into the streets of the Western Addition, to seek shelter there. Quite a number, though, lined themselves along the west side of Van Ness to wait with the firemen for the arrival of the dynamite. Several blocks behind the homes across the way, flames leaped high against a turbulent background of smoke.

Schmitz looked along the wide street as far as he could see in either direction. He nodded with satisfaction. Most of the people were pouring into Van Ness to his south, meaning that the soldiers were working their way from south to north. That was good. The fires at the south were the ones now closest to Van Ness. The use of the dynamite would start there.

He frowned suddenly and pulled out his watch. It was now close to two o'clock. Where had the time gone? And where was the dynamite? Two hours had passed since he had ordered that a boat be sent for it.

2.

"Where is the dynamite?"

Schmitz's worried question was repeated countless times as the passing minutes left two o'clock behind. It was asked by firemen still on their feet and those coming awake. It was asked by soldiers as they moved steadily north, clearing one block after another along the narrowing strip between the approaching wall of flame and the waiting line of defense. It was asked by householders on the west side of Van Ness and in the streets immediately beyond as, in compliance with the Mayor's orders, they threw up their windows. And, whenever the question was asked, anxious eyes jumped to the burning skyline and saw that, in places, the fire was now less than two blocks away. If the dynamite did not arrive soon—perhaps in minutes—it would be of no use, for the flames would be licking at the very homes in which it was to be used. Gone would be the chance for a monster firebreak. Gone would be the hope of saving the western part of the city.

The question reached General Funston at Fort Mason, where he had established his headquarters. He galloped across town to the harbor to see what was causing the delay. There, biting down on his cigar in rage, he heard that, thanks to some mixup, a boat had not yet sailed for the East Bay. He immediately took over the tug *Slocum* and sent it hurrying on its way.

Even before the little General set out for the harbor, soldiers were finishing off the job of clearing the families out of the homes along the east side of Van Ness. They were grand homes, multistoried and expensively furnished, and the reactions of the people who had to leave them were varied. Often there were pleas to spare the places, often promises that the owners would somehow protect them from the oncoming inferno, often threats to sue the city and the Army for wanton destruction, and at least one threat made at gun point. A soldier slapped the pistol aside and herded the family outdoors.

Many of the occupants, though, departed wordlessly, often biting back tears. Soldiers later said that a number of families disappeared into the Western Addition without even a backward glance. Others got no farther than the opposite side of the street, where they stopped to await mutely the coming death of their homes.

Here and there, the soldiers ran into attitudes that they called heroic. In one mansion, a man looked slowly about his richly furnished living room. Then he shrugged, said, "All right, boys, blow her to blazes," and walked outside. In another, an elderly woman cut a canvas portrait of her family from its frame, rolled it up under her arm, allowed a soldier to help her into her coat and went out to her waiting carriage. In still another, one of the members of the Committee of Safety gently scolded his wife for her tears, saying that "what must be done must be done."

It is possible that the soldiers who entered the mansion of Mrs. Merrill, the vice-president of the San Francisco Red Cross, encountered the greatest courage of the day. She had been feeding refugees ever since the preceding afternoon, and now she looked up to be told that she had thirty minutes to gather up her belongings before leaving. John Castillo Kennedy, telling her story in *The Great Earthquake and Fire*, writes that she "gestured to the refugees who crowded the house and replied quietly, 'All right, but thirty minutes will give me time to feed them.' "

It was now past three o'clock, and most of the homes along the central and southern sections of the twenty-five-block stretch were cleared. But still there was no dynamite. And now, in places along the southern reaches of the street, the wall of fire was just a half-block distant. The flames raged high, their reflection bloodying the murky air. Their roar was deafening and their heat reached out to set firemen and spectators to gasping. The east side roof-tops began to smolder. All hope of using dynamite there evaporated. The people could only wonder how many minutes would pass before the street itself was aflame and the fire was across it.

Down at the O'Farrell Street intersection, just a few blocks from the ruins left by the north-of-Market arm of the Ham and Eggs fire, they got their answer immediately. Even before the east side of Van Ness itself went afire, sparks blew across the wide boulevard and settled in small patches of flame on the roof of St. Mary's, the Catholic cathedral. Two priests grabbed axes and climbed to the roof, where they chopped the burgeoning fires out of existence and flung the smoldering shingles to the sidewalk below. Firemen and spectators cheered. The west side of Van Ness was safe for a while longer.

Farther north, along the five-block stretch between Bush and Washington Streets, a group of firemen and soldiers came to a decision. Here, the wall of flame advancing from Nob Hill was still three to four blocks away, and the men said they must not waste another moment waiting for the dynamite. They must build a firebreak by another means. They agreed to start a backfire by igniting the homes on the east side of the street and then trying to douse them out before the arrival of the oncoming holocaust.

In *The Earth Shook and The Sky Burned*, William Bronson says that their method of backfiring was "simplicity itself." He writes: "They poured kerosene generously over the floors, lit it, then rushed out and broke windows with rocks and sticks to increase the draft. It took only moments for a house to become a torch."

Within half an hour, the whole east side of Van Ness along the five-block run was afire. Bronson adds: "The heat created by the process was, of course, as hot as the enemy fire coming down the hill. Some observers claimed that the backfiring added to the hazard." To that criticism, the soldiers and firemen replied, "What else could be done without dynamite?"

Now, in the late afternoon, the oncoming wall of flame closed in on the middle section of the twenty-five-block stretch. In one spot after another, it crashed out onto the east side of Van Ness in the six blocks between Sutter Street on the south and Clay Street on the north. Firemen whipped their engines over close to the fires and aimed their slender hoses at them. But the heat was too much for them. It turned the thin streams of cistern water and sewage to steam long before they reached the flame. It blistered the men's faces and drove deep into their lungs, taking their breath away. The firehorses plunged wildly in pain. The firemen retreated to the west side curbs.

The heat followed them and shot past them to crash into the houses at their backs. Here and there, windows cracked, some shattering. Paint began to peel from the fronts of the homes. Shrubs and plants wilted.

With the heat came showers of blood-red sparks. They landed on the firemen and burned little holes in their clothing and stung deep into their flesh. Cries of pain and fear went up from the spectators along the sidewalks; they had fallen back at the first onslaught of heat, and now many scurried into the side streets and hurried off to the safety of distant neighborhoods. Finally, after lashing at the crowds, the sparks settled on the homes. Instantly, rooftops and porches were flecked with small fires.

The homeowners had long expected this moment. Now, without hesitation, they ran angrily to meet it. They dipped coats and dresses and shirts and petticoats and sacks and blankets into buckets of water that they had hoarded since yesterday morning and slapped their way from one patch of fire to another. Housewives dashed through their front-of-the-house rooms, pulling down curtains and drapes hot to the touch. Husbands and sons hurried to their rooftops, some pushing their way up through attic trapdoors, others climbing ladders that had been set in place hours ago. Other family members carried personal belongings, furniture, kitchenware, bedding, clothing and food to rear windows and heaved them outside, where they (or as many as possible) would be collected and hurried off to safety when and if the homes dissolved into torches.

Many of the firemen sprang to the aid of the homeowners. They knew that there was not a single hope of beating down the wall of flame and that their only chance to prevent the spread of the fire was to keep the west side homes from going ablaze. They swung their hoses toward the smoking porches and peeling walls. They climbed to the roofs. They beat at the smoldering shingles with their axes. Those without axes pulled the shingles up with their bare hands and threw them to the yards below. No one spoke; the searing heat made breathing all but impossible. And men wasted no breath on words. The inferno glow from across the street turned faces into blood-red masks. Far to the west, far beyond the two-mile-thick layer of smoke blanketing the city, the sun moved slowly down to the rim of the Pacific. It was five thirty.

At about that time, the tug *Slocum* pushed its nose in against the dock at Fort Mason up at the northern tip of Van Ness. The little ship lay low in the water, for every inch of her deck space was crammed with the barrels and crates of dynamite obtained from the East Bay. Soldiers, ordered to dockside more than an hour ago by General Funston, hurriedly transferred them to a half-dozen Army

wagons. By six o'clock, the wagons were far down Van
Ness, threading their way among firemen, spectators, hoses
and fire engines.

The firemen working in the six-block stretch between
Sutter and Clay Streets threw up their hands in exaspera-
tion when they saw the dynamite. They gathered about
the wagons and shouted that the stuff had arrived too late
to be of any value here. It would be better, they said, to
cart it back up Van Ness, back up the northern arm of the
fires coming in from Nob Hill, and use it there. The
wagon drivers stared at the towering flames across the
street and nodded in grim agreement.

But before the rigs could be turned about, several Army
and fire officers came shoving their way through the surrounding crowd and ordered that the dynamite be driven
one block west, over to Franklin Street. It was to be used
there in a new plan to stop the fire.

The wagon drivers obeyed without a question. But the
haggard, blackened firemen made up for their silence.
What new plan had been hatched? Why take the dynamite
to Franklin? What was going to happen now? They had
the sinking feeling that they knew the answers even while
they were asking the questions.

The answers were simple—and expected. The plan had
been formulated just minutes ago. It was based on the
hard fact that the fire could not be stopped along Van Ness
between Sutter and Clay. It was just a matter of time before it jumped the wide street. And so the dynamite was to
be used to build a new firebreak—this one along the east
side of Franklin for the six blocks between the Sutter and
Clay intersections.

The firemen nodded dumbly, certain that the new dynamiting would do no good. The oncoming flames would

simply leap across the roadway in an instant. The street was *so* narrow, so hopelessly narrow. The men felt that they were doomed to nights and days of falling back, one block at a time, in the face of the raging flames until at last they stood in the Pacific surf; only then would this nightmare end. But they did not protest the idea of the Franklin firebreak. They were too tired and, anyway, it was, they knew, all that could be done.

And so it was that, as night closed down all around, soldiers repeated a scene that had been played too often in San Francisco since yesterday morning. They raced along the east side of Franklin, clearing one building after another of occupants and driving refugees and spectators from every cross-street and intersection between Sutter and Clay. Behind them came demolition teams. Charges were set. The crash of explosions sent fresh black smoke rolling skyward to blot out momentarily the red glow from Van Ness.

As the night deepened, the flames jumped Van Ness at points all along the Sutter-Clay strip and gnawed their way toward the new rubble on Franklin. At the Sacramento Street intersection, just one block south of Clay, flying sparks crossed the wide boulevard and ignited a stable on the grounds of the Spreckels estate; shortly thereafter, the great main house went afire. Reports of the night say that the firemen there broke into tears when the flames got into the mansion. The place was built of stone and was reputedly fireproof. They had hoped that it would be able to hold the fire at bay at this one point on Van Ness.

Then, as midnight came and went, a strange feeling began to grow in all the firefighters up and down the six-block stretch. For hours now, they had fought the flames blindly, using any weapons at hand—blankets, cistern and bathtub water, sewage, axes, rakes, even bottles of wine; now they looked up and made a startling discovery: the fires had not yet managed to jump narrow Franklin. The men realized that somehow they were doing the impossible, and they identified the alien feeling in themselves. It was hope, hope that at last they might be getting the upper hand.

It was not until days later, not until they had the chance to compare notes, that they understood why the battle had turned in their favor somewhere in the midnight hours. They learned that three unexpected circumstances had come to their aid.

First, there was the Spreckels mansion, set in the middle of its great yard. Though its every room was ablaze, it was succeeding as a firebreak after all. Its massive stone shell was holding the flames within itself, frustrating their every attempt to lick out toward Franklin.

Second, north of Clay, water was beginning to return to a hydrant here and there, and firemen were putting it to use. Repair crews has worked continuously since yesterday morning at the shattered pipes leading to the Pilarcitos and Crystal Springs reservoirs. Their efforts were just now starting to pay off.

Finally, there was San Francisco's always-capricious wind. After changing direction several times since the quake—often helping the fires along, sometimes hindering them—it was now steadily blowing eastward from the Pacific. It was putting up a shield through which the flames could not advance.

By dawn Friday, the hope that was in the firemen had blossomed into exultation. The fires had been restrained from jumping Franklin and were beginning to die down.

They could be safely said to be under control here. On top of all this came heartening word from north of Clay: the flames sweeping in off Nob Hill, though they had reached Van Ness along a front of six blocks up to Green Street, had been unable to cross the boulevard because of the eastward-running wind.

The firemen could now tell themselves that the vast western area of San Francisco was safe. It seemed more miracle than fact.

But the news from north of Clay was good and bad all at the same time. True, the wind had kept the flames from jumping Van Ness, but it had accomplished something just as dangerous. It had turned them about, and now they were spreading north and east—up the sides of Russian Hill and toward Telegraph Hill, the North Beach area and the northern docks. San Francisco's western districts were safe. But now the crowded northeastern section was threatened.

It was a fair and evil trade.

3.

And what of the great fire plunging down through the Mission District below Market? How were things faring there?

By nightfall Thursday, the situation looked as hopeless as any to be found in San Francisco.

All through the day, the inferno had advanced steadily south along its ragged five-block-wide front—from Howard Street on the east to Dolores on the west. Without pause, it had jumped Thirteenth, Fourteenth and Fifteenth Streets. It had leveled hundreds of the modest

frame homes that were the hallmark of the district. It had
destroyed the Southern Pacific Hospital just a short while
after the patients there were transferred by wagon and car
to the Presidio. It had driven 50,000 people to the surrounding hills.

But the day had not been without some triumphs for the
firefighters. Somehow, they had managed the major feat of
keeping the fire from leaping its east and west boundaries;
had they not, it would have raced eastward back to the
remaining unburned blocks south of Market and would
have threatened the heavily populated Potrero District; on
the west, it would have burned into other neighborhoods
of the Mission and might well have swung north for an
attack on the Western Addition.

Too, at Sixteenth and Dolores, the firemen had kept it
from getting into the ancient adobe building that was Mission Dolores. They took great pride in this accomplish-
ment, for the mission had a special historical significance
for San Francisco. It was one of the oldest buildings in
town, and the saint in whose honor it had originally been
built—St. Francis of Assisi—was responsible for San Francisco's name. The mission later was given its present name.

At midevening, exhausted fire officers gathered on
Twentieth Street. The burning front was now just two or
three blocks away and was fast bearing down on them.
They agreed that they must set up a firm defense line
here and that it just might have a chance of success. From
where they stood, they could see three factors in their
favor. First, the street was fair-to-middling wide. Second,
there was some open ground and sturdy Mission High
School over on the west side of the Dolores intersection;
they could serve as pretty good firebreaks. Finally, and
most heartening of all, there was a large cistern up a

nearby hill, putting within reach at last the water they had needed so badly this day.

Their first step in setting up their defense line was to dynamite the buildings all along the north side of Twentieth. Then they hustled all their engines and horses to the foot of the hill on which the cistern was located. The street rising to the cistern was choked with spectators, and while drivers positioned their rigs for the uphill dash, firemen hurried into the crowd to break open a path. At last, the engines were waved forward.

Reins were snapped down hard. The engines jolted onto the hillside. For an instant or two, they moved swiftly to the cheers of the crowd. But then, abruptly, the speed and lurch went out of them. They slowed and stopped and began to slide downhill while their horses bucked and reared against their traces. Drivers shouted and cursed, but not in anger. Pity was what they felt. They knew that the horses, awake and on their feet for as long a time as any man here, just did not have the strength left to get the engines up the hill.

The consternation along the sloping roadway was not permitted to last more than a moment. Firemen dashed to the engines, unharnessed the teams, and began pushing the rigs toward the cistern. Officers shouted for help from the spectators. Before the words were out of their mouths, dozens of men, women and children came rushing forward. The engines were run up the hill, as one fireman later recalled, "in a twinkling."

The fire front reached Twentieth Street sometime after midnight. There, it ran into a determined line of firemen and citizens with axes, blankets, and—blessing of all blessings—effective hoses.

It went no farther.

**4.**

At dawn Friday, the great pall of smoke that had lain over San Francisco for two days and two nights seemed to be thinning. Refugees in the far western parks and streets looked at the sky and breathed a little easier. It gave truth to the many word-of-mouth reports that the fires along Van Ness and down in the Mission District were under control and dying down.

For the people of northeastern San Francisco, however, the morning was anything but a happy one. The pall of smoke was thickest over their section of the city. Thanks to the very eastward-blowing wind that had saved the Western Addition, the flames were now tearing toward their neighborhoods on Russian and Telegraph Hills and in the North Beach area.

Russian Hill, directly north of Nob Hill and much closer to Van Ness than was Telegraph Hill, stood in the greatest immediate danger this morning. Its southern and western slopes had been burned yesterday by the flames sweeping in off Nob Hill; now the fire was roaring back from Van Ness to blacken its northern and eastern sides.

Firemen and soldiers hurrying to the hill found that a number of householders had already done a fine job of firefighting. Immediately after the quake, they had filled their bathtubs and sinks with water still remaining in the city's shattered underground pipes. Then, when the great red stain had spread down from Nob Hill and had started up their own hill, they had wet down their homes and had extinguished every falling spark they could find. At one point, they had even plastered a house with wet sand barrowed in from a nearby construction site. The result was that several middle-class homes in an area one block wide and a little more than two blocks long at the crest of the hill were still unburned.

The new arrivals were eager to see that the hilltop remained undamaged. Flames were closing in fast, and a contingent of soldiers looked about to choose a home to protect. Their eyes came to the roof of a nearby house. What they saw there, along with the action it caused them to take, added up to one of the most often-repeated stories to come out of the day.

The home was owned by Eli T. Sheppard, who had departed yesterday to take his ailing wife to the safety of the East Bay. Remaining behind was elderly E. A. Dakin, a Civil War veteran who rented several rooms in the house. Dakin spent the night near a flagpole on the roof, watching the advance of the flames from Nob Hill. Now, with daylight here, they had come too close even for his tough old spirit. The shingles on the house were beginning to smolder, as were the trees down in the yard. He knew that he must get out immediately. But, before he left, he made one last gesture of defiance against the approaching holocaust. He brought out his great American flag and ran it to the top of the flagpole.

The soldiers looked at the rooftop just in time to see the flag unfurl in the smoke and wind. Reports of the day vary as to their reaction. Some hold that they thought the Sheppard house was a military headquarters. Others say that they decided such a gesture must not go unrewarded. Whatever their reaction, the result was their instantaneous decision to save the house at all costs.

As a man, they dashed up the hill and kicked in the door. Using bathtub water and even the contents of siphon bottles, they successfully defended the home until the fire swept away, leaving the hilltop unscathed. Over in the

East Bay, Sheppard and his wife heard the latest reports of the fires and were certain their home was gone. They returned a week later, to gape in surprise when they saw it still standing. A smiling and still defiant Dakin was on hand to greet them.

North and east of Russian Hill, the flames crashed on through street after street. On the north side, they fanned out over the hills and down into the North Beach district, en route to where the northeastern shore met the Bay. Likewise, on the east side, they spread up to North Beach while steadily rolling eastward to Telegraph. The thump of dynamite was heard every few minutes from all over the wide area as desperate bands of men tried to build firebreaks. The heat was too great for many exhausted firemen, soldiers and volunteer citizen workers. They collapsed and had to be carried away in wagons or in the arms of friends. And there were some who looked at the fire and said it would not be stopped until it had ravaged the whole northeastern section and had burned right back to its starting point in the produce section, where it would finally run out of fuel. They quietly threw down their firefighting tools and walked away to find a place to sleep.

Several blocks to the north of the Sheppard house stood another home that was to be spared that day, even though all else about it was leveled. Resembling a miniature castle at the corner of Lombard and Hyde Streets, it was the home of Robert Louis Stevenson's widow. Fittingly, it was saved by one of the most literary and artistic firefighting crews ever assembled.

The crew was made up entirely of writers, artists, sculptors, musicians, newsmen and cartoonists. All were members of the city's Press and Bohemian Clubs, and there probably wasn't an hour's worth of professional firefight-

ing experience in the whole lot. All they had on their side
was the determination that had welded them together earlier today for their journey through littered streets to this
blazing intersection—the determination to save a home so
full of literary tradition.

While fire raged on all sides, they carried water down
from an almost empty cistern on the slopes of Russian
Hill, dipped blankets in it, and successfully slapped away
every blaze that erupted in the house and on its roof. Mrs.
Stevenson was on a trip to Mexico at the time, and so was
not on hand to see the heroic work. Like the Sheppards,
she returned to San Francisco with the certainty that her
home was in ruins, only to find it still standing—battered
and charred, but still standing, thanks to that most un-
likely of fire crews.

By midafternoon, all of the sprawling North Beach section was gone. The last of its inhabitants—and they num-
bered in the thousands—had abandoned their homes and
shops. They had worked their way past the as-yet-
unburned northern side of Telegraph Hill to the harbor
and had turned south. Some headed for the Ferry Building
and a trip across the Bay to safety. Others made for Market
Street and the long hike through ashes and rubble out to
the Western Addition.

At the northeastern edge of the city, a point of the fire
came up against the Bay. From there, the burning front
stretched down and slightly back along an irregular line to
the western foot of Telegraph Hill. On reaching the Bay,
the point of fire started to follow the shoreline south, wid-
ening itself as it went. In its path lay the northern slopes
of Telegraph Hill to one side and the start of the docks to
the other.

Had there been panic on Telegraph Hill at that moment, it would have been understandable. Raging flames were now coming in from the east and north on a place that was built like a tinder box. Its slopes and crest were jammed with everything from shanties to houses to apartments—all of them constructed of wood. They were jammed so close together and the sides of the hill were so steep that often the only passages from one building to another were rope ladders and wood stairways. So far as fire was concerned, the hill was the city's least defensible place.

But there was no panic—just simple determination. Hundreds of men, all of them residents of the hill, were assembled there now, their faces hard as they watched the advancing red stain. For the most part, those faces were dark-skinned, for Telegraph Hill was home to much of San Francisco's Italian, Spanish and Mexican population. Hours ago, the men had sent their women and children away. Now, they were determined to save their modest homes at any cost.

They had made a good job of their preparations. Buckets lined the streets, all of them filled with water from a nearby cistern. Blankets, sacks, drapes and even old clothing were piled alongside them, as were axes, picks, shovels, brooms and rakes. Ladders were set against buildings. Some men had even placed bottles of wine and olive oil on their front porches; any sort of liquid might be needed for the coming fight. Sailors had stretched a hose clear up from the Bay, about a mile's worth of it.

To the north of the waiting men, the fire came through an area of warehouses, small factories and lumberyards. On the east, it ignited the remaining blocks in front of the hillside. Heat, so terrible that it took the breath away, reached out to the men. They fell back a step, now fright-

ened, angry and still determined all at the same time—
frightened because they were looking at the worst kind of
death; angry because, after moving far away from their
homes yesterday and last night, the fire had returned to
devour them. Gluttonous. There was no other word for
it.

Then the time for waiting and thinking ran out. Shortly
after five o'clock, the buildings on the lower northern
slopes began to smolder in the heat. The men ran to them.
They climbed ladders and ripped up smoking bits of tar-
paper roofs. They threw buckets of water against outer and
inner walls from which the heat was peeling paint and
colorful wallpaper. They pulled down flimsy curtains that
suddenly turned brown and burst into flame.

A yell went up from the north side. The fire was finally
on the hill. A cluster of little houses, some no better than
shanties, were burning. Bucket brigades moved in on
them. Several men screamed as burning embers fell on
them. One old man fainted in the heat. He was carried
uphill to safety. What safety?

Above and to the sides of the burning houses, others
began to smoke. They were little places, anchored into the
sharply rising hillside by means of wooden stilts, and they
would catch any minute now. Someone yelled for ropes.
They were brought on the run and lashed to the stilts.
Men pulled hard, saw the stilts break away and plunged
off in all directions as the houses crashed down about
them, splintering and tossing furniture everywhere. Back
to the ruins they came to haul timbers and planks and
household goods away from the flames.

But while they worked, the fire leaped uphill to other
buildings. New bucket brigades appeared. Water, wine,
olive oil, sewage—anything liquid—was tossed on the

flames. At one point on the northern slope, the sailors aimed their mile-long stretch of hose at the inferno. Then, in horror, they saw that the fire was circling them. They threw down the hose and ran for their lives.

Night came, intensifying the red-yellow glow and giving a deeper black to the rolling smoke. Some men arrived at newly threatened houses on the northern slopes. These places, too, stood on stilts, but the men had no ropes for the job of pulling them down. They did have axes, and so they began hacking away at the slender supports. They worked until they heard the houses begin to creak over-head and looked up to see them swaying drunkenly. Then they ran. The houses fell in the next seconds. Close-by, other men were reducing several tiny places to splinters with their axes and picks.

The hours moved toward midnight. The men worked without halt, without thought of exhaustion; for the most part, they were laboring men, accustomed to physical toil. And who thinks of exhaustion when his life and home are at stake? They ran their buckets back and forth between the cistern and the flames. They pulled down more threat-ened houses or pounded them to bits. Now and again, they paused to look down at the harbor. The flames coming in from the north, the very flames that were eating into their hill, were also fast approaching the first of the docks.

But now water was running low and the fire was flaring viciously in some newly struck houses on the northern slopes. Several men ran off, leaving their friends to fight the flames as best they could with their remaining blankets and buckets. Minutes later, whooping loudly, they re-turned, rolling casks of wine in front of them, casks plucked from some nearby cellar. The casks were split open and the wine spilled out over the flames.

Friday turned into Saturday, and the hours moved toward the dawn. The men began to look up and feel the very same astonishment that had touched the Van Ness firefighters twenty-four hours earlier. They could see that they were winning their battle. The fire, though it had advanced a goodly distance up the northern slopes, was still far short of the crest. It was no longer moving swiftly, hungrily. It had slowed almost to a halt. Ahead of it were a growing number of vacant lots. Spent as it seemed to be, it would never get past them. And over on the west, it had been held back right at the base of the hill, hardly making any encroachment at all on the slopes.

The men grinned and pounded each other on the back, their teeth flashing in the red glow. The fire still burned, but they could control it. Their hill was safe—battered but safe.

It was four o'clock in the morning, and the men on Telegraph Hill could relax a bit. But not the firefighters down the slopes to the east. There, the last arm of the fires that had started almost seventy hours ago in the produce section was still alive and full of fury. It was approaching the start of the harbor.

Falling back from it step by step were several exhausted fire companies. Just offshore, a little fleet of fireboats and tugs poured tons of Bay water onto it.

The fire reached out toward the Lombard Street pier, the northernmost of the wharves, and the firefighters groaned. If the flames got a good foothold here, they could sweep for miles down the city's eastern face, wiping out its every wharf and shipyard. The men were already thinking of San Francisco's recovery from the tragedy of these past three days. Loss of the harbor would slow that recovery immeasurably.

But the flames were not allowed to take hold of the pier. The firemen fought them back at the adjoining brick sheds. The tugs shot their tons of water in from the Bay. Slowly, so very slowly as the dawn broke, the life went out of the fire.

The holocaust of three days was at an end.

The time was seven o'clock in the morning. The day was Saturday, April 21.

# Chapter Ten

# REBIRTH

## 1.

FLAMES LINGERED IN THE RUINS throughout Saturday. Their strength waned with each passing hour. Now and again, here and there behind gaping windows and broken granite, they tried to flash with their old fury. But it was no use. They were gorged and, like all gluttons, were ready to sleep, and sleep to them meant death. At last, late in the night, the rain that had been needed for so long began to fall. The last strong glow went out of the ruins. The ash turned to thick, black mud.

After that, though some debris smoldered for weeks, the smoke cleared and San Francisco looked at her wounds. They were the worst ever inflicted on an American city.

Destroyed were 497 city blocks covering 2831 acres. Twenty-eight thousand buildings were gone—everything from shanties to modest homes to apartments and hotels to some of the finest mansions in the world; everything from the smallest and darkest pawnshops to the most pretentious offices, banks, shops and department stores; everything from the dustiest print shop to the city's tallest structure, the *Call* Building; everything from saloons and gambling dens to churches and thirty schools. Pick anything—theaters, restaurants, hospitals, drugstores, markets, libra-

ries, candy shops, police stations, art gallaries, museums—
they were gone. A quarter of a million people were homeless, and no one knows how many more were burned out of
their jobs or businesses. The fortunes of some of the
town's richest families, with its greatest property owners,
were wiped out.

Gone, too, was the transportation system—the trolleys
and the little cable cars, along with their main offices, repair shops and carbarns; their tracks, broken or wrenched
out of line or torn loose from the ground by the quake, lay
buried beneath tons of rubble. Telephone and electric
lines were melted away. Lampposts that had turned
molten in the inferno heat were arched over on their sides.
Countless thousands of city records had become ash.

These were the wounds. They had to be cleansed and a
new city had to be built on them.

In a way, stunned as they were, the people of San Francisco were ready as early as Friday for the massive work of
rebuilding. Their battered and bruised spirits took a sharp
turn upward that day when they learned that the fires had
been stopped at Van Ness. They began to think that, at
least, the whole city wasn't going to be wiped out.

Still higher went their spirits on Sunday. That was the
day on which an exhausted but triumphant Mayor wrote
out this proclamation and had it distributed throughout
town:

TO THE CITIZENS OF SAN FRANCISCO

The fire is now under control and all danger is passed.
The only fear is that other fires may start should people
build fires in their stoves until the chimneys have been
inspected and repaired properly. All citizens are urged to
discountenance the building of fires. I congratulate the
citizens of San Francisco upon the fortitude they have

displayed and urge upon them the necessity of aiding the authorities in the work of relieving the destitute and suffering.

The spirits of the people could not help but leap high. They now knew as fact what they had suspected Friday. Great sections of the city had been spared. The authorities —who had a bird's eye view of the whole thing—said so. There would be something left with which to start afresh. Something to build upon.

And so they were able to do what is required of any people who hope to rise from the wreckage of what had once been their homes. They made themselves as comfortable as possible in the ruins. They put on a happy, defiant face. They got on with the job of staying alive until the rebuilding could begin.

Cooking was the first order of the day. In all the unburned streets and parks, refugee women and their daughters gathered bricks and fashioned them into little fireplaces, joined by women who still had homes but who would not cook inside them in deference to Schmitz's appeal; across the tops of the little fireplaces they placed grates or metal sheets as cooking surfaces. Now and again, wood stoves were carted out from abandoned, half-collasped homes and put to use. The women also collected kitchen utensils, plates and silverware from unburned neighborhoods. Until relief supplies began to pour in, they shared whatever food was at hand. They scouted up tubs for baths and laundry when the water came back. They took care of each other's children.

The fathers and sons set to the job of building family shelters. First, they built tents of blankets, sheets and drapes. Then they pulled strips of wood from the ruins and fashioned them into tiny kitchens to keep the ash and street dust away from the fireplaces. In and about their makeshift quarters they placed bits of furniture borrowed or offered in great quantities from surrounding homes; rocking chairs, cushions, kitchen chairs and tables of all sorts appeared everywhere. After that, the men prowled through the smoking ruins in search of any canned food that the fires might have overlooked. Occasionally, some found what they were looking for.

The defiance and good cheer in the stricken city were quickly seen in the tents and hut kitchens as many a family decorated them with humorous signs. Above the doorway of one kitchen a husband printed in white paint "Hoffman Cafe"; on its side he wrote in smaller letters, "Cheer Up, Have One On Me." On the front of a family tent, built of tar paper and wood slats and window drapes, hung this sign: "Ring The Bell For Landlady—Furnished Rooms With Running Water Steam Heat And Elevator." Somebody else dreamed up "Eat, Drink And Be Merry, For Tomorrow We May Have To Go To Oakland."

Possibly the sign that spoke most eloquently of the city's defiance and determination to grow again was a poem that was tacked to the side of a rubbled building on Market Street. It read:

> The cow is in the hammock
> The cat is in the lake
> The baby in the garbage can
> What difference does it make?
> There is no water and still less soap
> We have no city, but lots of hope.

Though their spirits rose steadily from Friday to Sunday, the people knew full well that their situation remained desperate. They had survived the catastrophe, but there was always the fear of further quakes, deadly aftershocks; this fear jammed the street and park camps not only with the homeless but those who refused to go back inside their still-standing homes lest the walls and ceilings come down in a fresh convulsion. Food, clothing, tents, bedding and medicine were in short supply—especially food. The soldiers and police had collected as much food as possible for rationing, and Mayor Schmitz's Committee of Safety had taken over its distribution, but there had been barely enough to go round to begin with, and now it had almost disappeared. There was still little or no water. With countless people bunched together in the streets and with corpses lying in the ruins, there was the constant and terrible threat of disease. The knowledge of these many hazards added thousands to the number that had already fled the city. The authorities hurried them on their way, encouraging any and all to leave. The fewer people who remained, the easier the job of recovery.

Then, sometime Saturday, aid from the outside world began to arrive.

The aid came in a mounting flood that reached tidal wave proportions by early the following Monday. It continued to pour in unabated for weeks to come. It arrived from throughout the United States and from fourteen foreign nations. In all, it added up to almost $10,000,000 in cash and goods.

The flow actually started on the day of the quake. It began with that trainload of medical supplies and personnel assembled in Los Angeles for shipment north. It started with Secretary of War Taft's order for those 200,000 rations from Vancouver Barracks and for all the available tents from Army posts round the country. It

started with President Roosevelt's request to Congress for
$500,000 in relief funds.

After that, as word of the disaster spread throughout the
civilized world, the floodgates opened. Stepping forward
quickly to help were:

•

American cities and states—Los Angeles gathered
seventy-five more freight cars worth of food and cooking
gear. New York collected $185,000 from its people and
immediately used $60,000 of that amount for a shipment
of drugs, following it with food and clothing. Ogden,
Utah, donated practically every loaf of bread baked there
for days. California's capital city, Sacramento, sent laden
riverboats down to the stricken city. The state of Massa-
chusetts drew $500,000 from its treasury.

•

Foreign nations—Japan, herself often the victim of
earthquakes, contributed $244,910 through her govern-
ment and Red Cross. The Dowager Empress of China donated $40,000. Canada came forward with $145,412 from
her people, France with $21,235, Mexico with $14,480 and
England with $6,570. Smaller amounts were raised in
other countries—$734 in Cuba, $385 in Australia, $199 in
Russia, $32 in Ceylon and $50 each in Scotland, Belgium,
Austria, Germany. A total close to $475,000 came from all
these countries.

•

Individuals—The most famous theatrical personalities of
the day participated in fund-raising shows and stunts for
the city. In New York, song-and-dance man George M.
Cohan sold newspapers for up to $1000 a copy. Actress

Sarah Bernhardt gave several benefit performances, as did Marie Dressler and other stage and silent motion picture stars. In Los Angeles, heavyweight boxing champion Jim Jeffries raised $600 by selling a crate of oranges at $20 an orange.

•

Organizations—Salvation Army workers appealed for funds in cities across the nation. In New York, the Metropolitan Opera, whose touring company was in San Francisco at the time of the quake, gave a benefit performance. The Barnum and Bailey Circus donated $20,000—the sum of one day's receipts. The American National Red Cross immediately asked Mayor Schmitz what sort of help was most urgently needed and then sent workers into the city. The United Brotherhood of Carpenters and Joiners of Indianapolis contributed $10,000.

•

The United States Government—No sooner had he asked Congress for $500,000 in relief funds than President Roosevelt upped the ante to $1,000,000. Congress approved the request and then added additional funds until $2,500,000 had been earmarked for San Francisco. Weeks later, Roosevelt told the city that it could have as much as $20,000,000 in federal monies to help rebuild itself.

It must be said here that not everyone gave freely to the city's relief. While most people regarded San Francisco as a place of great charm and shared in a very human sorrow for her plight, there were those who thought she had gotten exactly what she deserved in the earthquake and fire. They looked on her not as a great young seaport and a cosmopolitan city in love with her theaters, art galleries, restaurants and fine mansions. They saw her, rather, as a place of sin long in need of a Divine spanking, a place where there was gambling, where such wicked things as the opium dens of Chinatown and the saloons of the Barbary Coast were permitted to flourish, where the city government was corrupt, where far too many people stayed up far too late going to the theater and dining and dancing and drinking, a place where the peoples of too many races and too many colors mingled freely.

The outsiders who saw her this way rejoiced. The Good Lord had attended to her badness. One religious group in the Middle West was so jubilant that it held a celebration complete with brass band.

There were a goodly number of people inside the city who felt the same way. Providence, they were quick to say, had dealt her a long-overdue blow; perhaps now she would change her ways. But these people were in the minority, both inside and outside the city. Most San Franciscans scoffed at them or ignored them, saying that her faults were those of any city where thousands of peoples lived and particularly one that was young and fast growing. She was a frisky youngster and she liked a good time, and it was pretty archaic and mean to believe that God went around knocking down everything and everybody He disliked. Anyway, there was a sound natural reason for the earthquake that had triggered the whole mess. Remember the San Andreas fault?

One San Franciscan, on hearing the talk that the earthquake and fire had been Divine punishments, recollected that he had come upon a saloon standing unburned in a block otherwise leveled. He sat down and wrote a little verse. It reflected the attitude of most San Franciscans.

> If, as some say, God spanked the town
> For being over-frisky
> Why did He burn the churches down
> And save Hotaling's whisky?

By the first of the new week, tons of supplies were arriving in the city. Hundreds of tents were immediately pitched in the Presidio and Golden Gate Park; families were quickly assigned to them, thus relieving the congestion in the streets. Blankets and clothing were distributed throughout town. Medicines were divided among hospitals and aid stations.

Of all the relief supplies, food arrived in the greatest quantity. So much of it poured in that the fear of famine, ever present in the first post-quake days, was soon forgotten. Distribution stations—there were more than 175 of them at one time—were set up. Thousands of people thronged about them daily, forming into long lines for rations of bread, vegetables, meat, coffee and canned goods.

Everyone in town got into the lines at one time or another. The rich and the poor, the illustrious and obscure all stood there together and rubbed shoulders. Reports of the time say that everyone received equal treatment, regardless of their former social standing. They say, too, that very few ever asked for preference. Patience and good humor were evident everywhere.

This time of equality—and the good cheer with which San Franciscans greeted it—inspired Charles K. Field to pen one of the most popular verses to come from the quake and fire. Written from the standpoint of a housewife of humble means, it reads:

An' Mrs. Van Bergen she greets me these days
With a smile an' a nod of the head;
"Ah, Mrs. McGinnis, how are you?" she says,
"An' do you like Government bread?"
She fetches a bag made of crockydile skin
An' I've got a sack when we meet,
But the same kind of coffee and crackers goes in,
An' it's all of it cooked in the street.
Sure Mrs. Van Bergen is takin' it fine,
Ye'd think she was used to the food;
We're gettin' acquainted a-standin' in line,
An' it's doin' the both of us good.

The distribution stations, along with a string of hot
meal kitchens subsequently established, handed out as
much as 1,400,000 pounds of food a day during the first
weeks of their operation. The Red Cross reported that it
served 313,000 meals on April 30. Then, as food again
became available for sale, the number of people in the
lines fell off to 225,000 by May 10. By July, there were
only about 20,000 needy still receiving food.

In charge of the tidal wave of relief supplies at first was
Mayor Schmitz's Committee of Safety. The exhausted
Mayor found himself working as hard as, if not harder
than, during the disaster itself. There was work to be done
day and night to see that the supplies, starting to come in
at the rate of about 150 freight cars daily, were received
and dispersed. On top of this were all the problems of
getting city services back on their feet, of tending the ill
and injured and of pumping some business life back into
the town.

To do all these jobs, the Mayor broke the committee
down into subcommittees and then kept a sharp eye on
their work. In all, there were thirteen subcommittees. The

titles bestowed on them indicate the wide range of their work and their attempt to care for every single need in the city. There were committees to feed the hungry, to find housing for the homeless, to supervise the distribution of drugs and medical supplies, to attend to the injured and sick, to arrange for the transportation of people leaving the city, to help the homeless of Chinatown and to restore electric power, telephones, water and retail trade.

Worn and busy as he was, Schmitz must have had his moments of pride and even happiness in those first days of recovery. He had seen his city through the disaster, putting aside his old greeds and forgetting his enemies to get the job done. He had shown qualities of genuine leadership. He had stayed on his feet when he should have collapsed. In the face of bitter opposition from some of the town's leading citizens, he had stood fast in his determination to build the Van Ness Avenue firebreak. Now he was doing his best to get San Francisco back on her feet. He was greeted as a hero wherever he went.

But with the quake and the fire now in the past, he was to take two slaps in the face. The first came from President Roosevelt.

Though Washington, D.C., was a long way from San Francisco, Roosevelt was aware of the city's long and sad history of political graft. Consequently, he decided not to entrust the tidal wave of relief supplies and funds to the town's officials. Rather, he said, the responsibility of supervising them should be given to the Red Cross. Dr. Edward T. Devine, a veteran of relief work in New York, was appointed to take charge on the scene.

A cry of outrage and disappointment was heard from San Franciscans when Devine's appointment was announced. Though they knew that Schmitz's administration had been corrupt, their pride was hit hard by the President's action. In a nutshell, their attitude was: What's the matter, don't you trust us? Don't you think we can handle our own affairs? Fortunately, Devine proved an excellent leader. Under his direction, the relief work moved forward swiftly and efficiently, earning him the respect of the entire city and drowning out its initial anger. In early May—with Devine and his Red Cross workers attending to all relief work and the Army in charge of protecting health and property—Schmitz's Committee of Safety was disbanded.

The second blow dealt Schmitz came early in 1907 when, as had been so long expected, he and his political boss, Abe Ruef, were brought to trial for graft. Ruef was sent to prison for five years. Schmitz was dismissed from office. His political life was at an end.

By that time, San Francisco was rebuilding itself.

## 2.

No date can be given to mark the exact start of San Francisco's reconstruction. The fact is that rebuilding started almost as soon as the big fires were out and while the ruins were still smoldering and pocked with small blazes. It is said that many merchants started to put up temporary quarters on their property while the tumbled wood there was still hot to the touch. Their impatience, incidentally, was in the tradition of the city, for, during the great fires of the Gold Rush days, saloonkeepers had been known to begin rebuilding their little establishments while the places were still going up in flames. It was a roaring boomtown in those days, and every wasted minute meant lost cash.

Within days of the disaster, businesses were setting themselves up in homes and all available office space throughout the unburned areas of the city. The great mansions along the undamaged stretches of Van Ness proved especially popular. Banks, law firms and stock-and-bond houses settled in, remaining there and carrying on "business as usual" until new buildings came into being. The post-quake days marked the beginning of great change for Van Ness—its gradual transformation from a grand residential avenue to the business street of glittering neon that it is today.

Most vital to the city's recovery were the banks. Their officers quickly brought back the money they had sent to safety early in the disaster. Then, immediately, they located themselves and got their doors open. Money returned to circulation. People could buy food. Businessmen could start to buy needed merchandise. The economic heart of the city started to beat again. It quickened and grew stronger when many bankers and stockbrokers who had been unable to get their money and stocks out of town opened the vaults in their ruined buildings and found their contents undamaged.

City officials sighed with relief when they found the street surfaces relatively undamaged beneath all the rubble. Likewise, they learned, the underground water and sewer pipes had for the most part suffered minor harm. Water had been unavailable during the fire mainly because the out-of-town pipes leading to the Pilarcitos and Crystal Springs reservoirs had been crushed. Mercifully, the same fate had not befallen most of the pipes inside the city. These strokes of good fortune would facilitate reconstruction.

What bothered everyone was the amount of rubble in

the streets. There were tons of the stuff. Rebuilding could not get in gear until it was removed from underfoot. The problem was solved by laying down temporary tracks from several parts of the downtown district to the city's northeastern shore. Little dump cars, all of them laden with debris, were run along the tracks night and day, depositing their loads in the bay and clattering back for more. Assisting them were gasoline trucks and horse-drawn wagons. The work continued unabated for months. By the time it was done, it had cost the city $20,000,000.

As each street was cleared, buildings of all sorts sprang up along it—department stores, shops, offices, apartments, restaurants, even theaters. The rebirth of the city's business was aided by insurance monies and the $2,500,000 in funds from the government.

In the months following the disaster, insurance companies began to pay off damage claims on the fire insurance policies written in the city—policies that totaled somewhere between $225,000,000 and $250,000,000. It was a staggering amount, and there were many companies that could not or would not discharge their responsibilities for fear of being driven bankrupt. Fortunately, though, most major companies honored their debts, either paying them in full or making reasonable adjustments. A dozen lesser companies collapsed when they met their obligations. A total of $167,000,000 in insurance payments was made. The money was immediately pumped into the rebuilding program.

It did not, could not, cover the total cost of damages to the city. They were estimated at between $350,000,000 and $500,000,000. But the money was of immeasurable help in getting life started afresh.

As for the government appropriation, it was spent on

both large and small businesses. Small businessmen and laborers were especially helped by it through a program of small assistance grants. The grants were used by laborers for the purchase of tools needed for their return to work and by small businessmen for supplies and merchandise.

Simultaneously, the government appropriation did much to relieve the plight of the homeless. With it, a number of barracks-like buildings were brought into the city to replace the tent dwellings. Soon thereafter, it financed the construction of 6000 little wood cottages of two and three rooms. All these buildings—barracks and cottages—were up in time for the winter rains of 1906.

The era of rebuilding was a time of employment for all. There were jobs for everyone, from the most common of laborers to the most skilled of craftsmen. The cleanup and construction went on round the clock seven days a week, and anyone who long persisted in taking the charity of relief supplies when he could pay his way with a job was soundly hooted by all around him. The city seemed to be a beehive of unending activity.

And the result of all that work?

By the beginning of May, the sewer and water systems were back in operation. Utility lines were repaired and most homes had their electric lights on by summer. Within three years, upwards of 20,000 of the 28,000 ruined buildings had been replaced, with the new buildings constructed of better materials. And, within three years, close to the entire destroyed area had been born anew.

The materials—and the workmanship—in the new buildings *had* to be of better quality so far as San Franciscans were concerned. Their city's history had passed a milestone—a frightful one—and they were determined not to come this way again. The child had learned its lesson.

From now on, a wary eye would always be kept on the terrible damage that wind-swept fires and the restless San Andreas fault could do. Strict construction standards were created and enforced. The fire department was rebuilt, new and improved equipment was purchased for it, more and more modern training techniques were put into effect as time passed, and it was set on its way to becoming the splendid organization that it is today. Finally, a water system was developed that would be adequate to meet any emergency. New pipes were installed wherever necessary, great reservoirs were built, and dozens of cisterns were dug beneath intersections throughout town.

Out of all the devastation, a modern city took shape.

And so it was that, with patience, good will and determination, San Francisco lifted herself from the rubble and ashes and began to live again.

Her heartbeat strengthened with every passing month. One by one, her various sections—Chinatown, the Mission District, the South of the Slot neighborhoods, Telegraph Hill, Nob Hill, Russian Hill, North Beach, and the financial, produce and retail areas—were made whole again, most of them coming back with a new vigor and an improved look. In just nine short years, she was able to welcome visitors from over the world to her Exposition of 1915 and show them that hardly a scar remained from her long ordeal and that, rollicking child no more, she was on her way to becoming the queen city that she is today.

As a queen this day, she is many things to many people: great seaport; financial center; industrial center; cultural center; siren call beckoning visitors from over the world; home to more than 600,000 men, women and children; and place of work to thousands more.

However they see her, they know her moods are myriad and varied, as befits a queen. On a sunny spring day, with her wind-washed air sparkling clear, she is serene. In the morning and early evening of any workday, when thousands of commuters jam her streets and entry ways with their clattering cars and buses, she is turbulent. At her opera, she is haughty, often self-consciously so. At her Candlestick Park and Kezar Stadium, she is a noisy, unabashed baseball and football fan. In the colors and accents of her peoples, she is cosmopolitan. In her tenements, she is forlorn; in her middle-class neighborhoods, comfortable and often grand; in her richest homes, always grand. With the fog of a July evening lying over her bay and obscuring her skyline and setting the foghorns on her Golden Gate Bridge to their deep-throated talk, she is mysterious. And, on any clear night, when the lights strewn across her shoulders glitter like a diamond with a million facets for those who watch from Vista Point on the northern shore of the Golden Gate, she is ever majestic.

But to those watchers who know her best there is always one understanding, clear and unmistakable. In the heart of hearts that lies beneath her maturity and majesty, she remains the joyful child that she was just one breath before 5:12:25 A.M., Wednesday, April 18, 1906.

Nothing, not even the San Andreas fault, can take that away from her.

# SELECTED READING

Bowlen, Frederick: *San Francisco Fire Department History*, San Francisco: *San Francisco Chronicle*: May 14-July 13, 1939

Bronson, William: *The Earth Shook, The Sky Burned*, Garden City, N.J.: Doubleday, 1959

——: *Still Flying and Nailed To The Mast*, Garden City, N.J.: Doubleday, 1963

Iacopi, Robert, *Earthquake Country*, Menlo Park, Calif.: Lane Books, 1964

Jackson, Charlotte, *The Story of San Francisco,* New York: Random House, 1955

James, Marquis and Bessie R., *Biography of a Bank: The Story of Bank of America,* New York: Harper, 1954

Kennedy, John Castillo, *The Great Earthquake And Fire: San Francisco, 1906,* New York: Morrow, 1963

Lewis, Oscar, *San Francisco: Mission To Metropolis*, Berkeley, Calif.: Howell-North, 1966

Lewis, Oscar and Hall, Carroll D., *Bonanza Inn*, New York: Knopf, 1939

O'Brien, Robert, *This Is San Francisco*, New York: Whittlesey, 1948

Older, Mrs. Fremont, *San Francisco, Magic City*, New York: Longmans, Green, 1961

Riesenberg, Jr., Felix, *Golden Gate*, New York: Knopf, 1940

Sutherland, Monica, *The Damndest Finest Ruins*, New York: Coward-McCann, 1959

Young, John P., *Journalism In California*, San Francisco: Chronicle Publishing Company, 1906

# INDEX

I